Cambridge Elements ≡

Elements in the Problems of God
edited by
Michael L. Peterson
Asbury Theological Seminary

THE PROBLEM OF DIVINE PERSONALITY

Andrew M. Bailey
Yale-NUS College

Bradley Rettler
University of Wyoming

CAMBRIDGE
UNIVERSITY PRESS

Shaftesbury Road, Cambridge CB2 8EA, United Kingdom

One Liberty Plaza, 20th Floor, New York, NY 10006, USA

477 Williamstown Road, Port Melbourne, VIC 3207, Australia

314–321, 3rd Floor, Plot 3, Splendor Forum, Jasola District Centre,
New Delhi – 110025, India

103 Penang Road, #05–06/07, Visioncrest Commercial, Singapore 238467

Cambridge University Press is part of Cambridge University Press & Assessment,
a department of the University of Cambridge.

We share the University's mission to contribute to society through the pursuit of
education, learning and research at the highest international levels of excellence.

www.cambridge.org
Information on this title: www.cambridge.org/9781009619233

DOI: 10.1017/9781009269254

When citing this work, please include a reference to the DOI 10.1017/9781009269254

First published 2024

A catalogue record for this publication is available from the British Library

ISBN 978-1-009-61923-3 Hardback
ISBN 978-1-009-26924-7 Paperback
ISSN 2754-8724 (online)
ISSN 2754-8716 (print)

The Problem of Divine Personality

Elements in the Problems of God

DOI: 10.1017/9781009269254
First published online: December 2024

Andrew M. Bailey
Yale-NUS College

Bradley Rettler
University of Wyoming

Author for correspondence: Andrew M. Bailey, wrathius@gmail.com

Abstract: The main question of this Element is whether God has a personality. The authors show what the question means, why it matters, and that good sense can be made of an affirmative answer to it. A God with personality – complete with particular, sometimes peculiar, and even seemingly unexplainable druthers – is not at war with maximal perfection, nor is the idea irredeemably anthropomorphic. And the hypothesis of divine personality is fruitful, with substantive consequences that span philosophical theology. But problems arise here too, and new perspectives on inquiry itself. Our cosmos is blessed with weirdness aplenty. To come to know it is nothing less than to encounter a strange and untamed God.

Keywords: personality, classical theism, theistic personalism, Trinity, personality traits, perfection, perfect being theology, theistic arguments, atheistic arguments

ISBNs: 9781009619233 (HB), 9781009269247 (PB), 9781009269254 (OC)
ISSNs: 2754-8724 (online), 2754-8716 (print)

Contents

1 Inception

1.1 Persons and Personality

Think of someone you love. What is she like? And more to the point: what is she like . . . as a person?

Trained philosophers might immediately rattle off various abstract features that are characteristic of people. They might say your friend is conscious, that she freely chooses for reasons, has a perspective on the world, believes or knows things, and so on. They might even comment on whether your friend is or has a body or soul. They'd say what your friend is like by saying what she is.

There is another and better reply – a reply that someone uncorrupted by philosophy might give. If you're of this happy persuasion, you might answer the question by speaking to your friend's personality – her dream life, her passion for lutes, her fear of yellow snakes, her preference for large dogs over small cats, her cautious approach to big choices, her love of wide open spaces, and so on. Such a reply would focus, not on features your friend shares with other people, but on the ones that set her apart. These don't make her better than other people, just different. The style of reply in view would also focus on her psychology – her mental life, in all its cognitive, affective, and appetitive glory. It would say *who* and not just what she is.

God is a person, some say. God is three persons, say others. Yet others say that God, despite not being a person, is somehow personal. And philosophers or theologians attracted to these slogans have long debated whether God is conscious, freely chooses for reasons, knows things, and so on. They have debated, that is, whether God has various features we generally expect people to have. These questions are well-trodden. But does God have a dream life? Favorite music? A passion for lutes? Peculiar fears or aversions? How does God feel about dogs versus cats? Is God cautious, risk-tolerant, or risk-seeking? What would it even mean for God to have a personality along these lines – and is supposing that there is indeed a divine personality consistent with other widely held views about God? These questions are much less well-understood and discussed. They are the centerpiece of the present study.

Before saying more about what these questions mean, why they matter, and how the rest of this volume will unfold, we'd like to comment on methodology – what we'll take for granted, and our general approach across the pages to come.

1.2 How to Think about God

In this study, we are going to think about God. We will reflect on what God might be like, or at least formulate some educated guesses on the matter. And we don't just want to reflect on *what* God might be; we also want to think about *who* God might be.

These goals face grave problems. Even among those who concur that God exists, there is extensive reasoned disagreement: on the questions that are appropriate to ask, on the tools by which to approach them, on which evidence is useful or relevant, on the role of tradition and authority, on the limits of inquiry, and on how philosophical theology and its abstruse doctrines should relate to religious practice.

We will not argue for the aptness of our own approach to philosophical theology, but we will comment on what it is.

In what follows, we shall operate within this constraint: we'll take it as given that there is a God, and that God is maximally perfect. We shall, furthermore, take God's perfection to include great – indeed, maximal – goodness, knowledge, and power.[1] Subsequent sections will explore what these features amount to, and whether or how they interact with the hypothesis that God has a personality. But divine perfection will remain an unargued background assumption.

Many of our arguments will make no appeal to special revelation. The evidential base on which we'll often draw shall be, if you like, that of pure and unaided reason rather than special revelation. None of this is in conflict, we trust, with devout allegiance to tradition or scripture or creed and the evidence they furnish; for our results will speak mainly to what the *other* evidence says. And for all we say, the full evidential picture – one that includes both special revelation and pure reason – may support different views than the ones we argue for here: a familiar limit to unaided philosophical theology, but no decisive reason to not do it. Our closing meditation, finally, will be firmly situated within the Christian tradition, and draw from its distinctive doctrine of the Trinity. We hope that the maneuvers on display there will serve as a useful model for philosophers from other traditions to draw from, when applying, developing, or disputing the hypothesis of divine personality.

We will aim at the direct presentation of novel ideas, furthermore, rather than commentary on the history of philosophical theology. So though we will occasionally draw explicit connections between our topics and more familiar ones, our main aim will be to chart a course into new territory and to do it our way. We'll avoid fancy vocabulary, variables, analytic machinery, and

---

[1] Nagasawa (2017).

detailed scholarly apparatus. Footnotes will be light and nondiscursive, and sometimes we'll elide distinctions that would command elaborate attention in an analytic philosophy article. We won't even use numbered premise-conclusion arguments, sticking instead to plain English prose. The resulting study will, we hope, be of interest to nonexperts and students at every level and readable even to those without much fondness for analytic philosophical theology.

We're going to be saying "perhaps" a lot, in the pages to come. This is apt, since our approach will be speculative in three ways. First, we will offer arguments that derive from premises that are uncertain; this is a consequence of relying on unaided reason – and perhaps a consequence of doing any theology at all. Our conclusions will fall short of full certainty and permit deep but reasonable disagreement. Neither our starting nor ending places command assent. Second, our approach will often concern what is *possible* given what is known rather than what is *true or most likely*, given what is known. We will seek hypotheses that are not ruled out by various constraints, that is, which is different from strictly deriving new truths from old ones. Third, and in accordance with the remit of the series in which this study appears, a main goal throughout will be to raise thorny new questions and vexing problems, rather than to identify clean answers or decisive solutions. There is room here, not just for problems, but for play. Where the intellectually cautious dare not tread, we will dance.

1.3 The Questions and Their Meaning

Here are two widely discussed questions about God. First: is God a person? Second: is God personal? These questions are controversial. Their contents – what it is they are even asking – are contentious, too. Here's our take – not on their answers, but on their meaning.

To ask whether God is a person is to ask whether God is an individual locus of consciousness, action, and propositional attitudes. And these predicates – *is conscious, acts, knows, believes*, and so on – are here taken to be univocal; they mean the same thing when applied to God as when saying of a human person that she is conscious, acts, or knows.

To ask whether God is merely personal, by contrast, is to ask whether God is an individual locus of consciousness, action, or knowledge only in a more extended, analogical, metaphorical, or equivocal sense. God may know things without being an individual locus of consciousness. Or at least, it might be true to say of something that God knows it without God being an individual locus of consciousness. God may have beliefs without being a person – or at least, "God believes that Abraham was faithful" may be true without God being a person. A God may be personal, then – conscious, acting, or knowing – in *some* sense of each of these, without being a person in the precise way that we are.

The paragraphs above are not the only way to explain the first two questions or what separates them. In contexts where the Christian doctrine of the Trinity is at issue, for example, variations on the second question sometimes concern divine persons and their relation to the divine essence. And not everyone who thinks God is a person accepts the univocity of predication about that predicate, or any other. But the paragraphs will do for now, and they prepare us to present a third question that is a focal point of this study: does God have a personality?

We will not offer a systematic account of what this third question means. It is not quite clear, after all, what we are saying when we say that a car, or dog – or human person – is endowed with personality. It isn't totally clear, furthermore, which kinds of traits comprise someone's personality, and which ones are more incidental. Nor are personality psychologists united in their understanding of those questions.[2] So instead of offering an exhaustive and exhausting account of what it is to have a personality or for it to comprise some traits (in the form of, say, perfectly general necessary and sufficient conditions), we will give examples of traits that would, if exemplified by God in sufficient quantity and degree, suffice for there being a divine personality.

As a first pass: to ask whether God has a personality is to ask whether God exemplifies enough traits like these:

- Peculiar aesthetic sensibilities – a preference for red flowers over blue, say
- General aesthetic sensibilities – a preference for simplicity or repetition over variety or ornate constructions, say
- Introversion or extroversion
- A desire to avoid conflict rather than seek it out, when possible
- A distinctive tolerance for (or aversion to) risk
- A distinctive time bias, or lack thereof – preferring things now over later, or vice versa, or not at all
- A distinctive tolerance for (or aversion to) uncertainty
- A peculiar communication style – a preference for communicating only in formal languages and in mathematically rigorous ways, say, or a preference for bombast or metaphor
- A standing disposition to communicate in riddles to large audiences and in explicit statements to just three individuals in particular

---

[2] Cloninger (2009).

- A distinctive sense of humor – being disposed to make a very specific kind of joke, for example, or finding puns decidedly unfunny in comparison to elaborate incongruity
- A preference for expressing love through gifts rather than words
- An inclination to work with larger groups rather than smaller ones – or individuals
- A preference to spend time with people whose names begin with "J"
- Appetite for play – preferring whimsical modes of communication or choice (using goofiness as a tie-breaker when faced with equally good or incommensurable options, for example)
- A preference to bestow benefits on descendants of a particular person–Abraham, say
- Being a fan of Everton Football Club – rejoicing when Everton win, bestowing special favor on star players, and despairing when, as is far more often the case, Everton lose
- A disposition to dwell on the distant past, not with longing or regret, but with special reflective appreciation not bestowed on the more recent past – a perfected form of nostalgia, we might say

Socratic strictures aside, defining a question by giving examples of possible answers to it is a fine path to take. And the examples given do help fix our attention on the focal phenomena of this study. But we can do more than just give examples; we can also observe their structure, and the ways they differ or resemble.

All of the examples given are broadly psychological. They involve mental states, whether cognitive or affective or appetitive. One might suspect that God can have a personality only if God is a person. To be a person, the idea goes, is to be an individual with sufficiently many mental capacities – for sophisticated conscious experience, cognition, affection, and appetite, say – and since the example traits in view all require those kinds of mental capacities, God enjoys them only if God is a person.

It's a tempting thought. But there are reasons to deny or be agnostic about it. One goes like this: although sentences which attribute particular thoughts or feelings to God are true, they are not to be taken univocally; and so they do not obviously entail a univocal attribution of personhood to God. At most, they suggest that God is merely personal. Another reason goes like this: personhood is a matter of having capacities, where capacities involve at least some unrealized potential. But, goes the thought, God's perfection precludes any unrealized potential at all; the fancy way of saying this is that God is pure act without any potency. Philosophers and theologians of this persuasion, we suspect, will resist any attribution of capacities to God, personhood-entailing, or otherwise. Although they may countenance the attribution of personality traits to God, they'll deny that such traits make God a person. And so, the line between personality and personhood needn't be so straight. God may have a personality without being a person. A final complication is that there is considerable disagreement about the connections, if any, between being personal, being a person, and many of the usual things believers say about God.[3] In cases like these, where even basic conceptual vocabulary is at issue, we think it can be productive to try on an alternative vocabulary and see how it goes. Thus, we will engage the question of divine personality without explicit commitment to divine personhood.

We take no stand just yet on whether normatively valenced features – psychological properties that are intrinsically good or bad to have – can be genuine elements of personality. And so by design our list does not include, for example, a disposition toward apt fidelity to friends and lovers (loyalty – a virtue), or a disposition toward excessively quick and careless evaluation of evidence (intellectual recklessness – a vice). And nothing much about what we have to say will hang on whether virtues and vices and such belong on the list. For, given our assumption that God is perfect, it seems dubious that vices would show up in the divine personality. And whether virtues show up isn't relevant to our inquiry either – we're much more interested in whether God has quirks and character than whether, say, God exhibits the virtue of justice.

Thus what the examples have in common. Now, a bit about what divides them.

Some of our examples concern quite general conditions or states of affairs. Being affectionate around and toward one's good friends is capacious in this way. We'll call these traits *dispositions*. Others concern particular created beings – by name, as it were. Being affectionate toward Lilith is rather more singular in this way. If you want to activate this trait, you'll need Lilith – and it won't be easy to aptly describe the trait without talking about Lilith herself. Some metaphysicians might say these traits are *haecceitistic*; we'll call them *druthers*.

It may be that all druthers are special cases of dispositions, or vice versa. Perhaps a positive attitude toward Abraham and his sons, for example, is in fact a point along a dimension (whether discrete or continuous), one far end of which is an extremely positive attitude toward Abraham, and the other far end of which is an extremely negative attitude toward Abraham. And there may be other systematic relations between these two broad trait classes as well. But we'll be

---

[3] Burns (2009).

neutral on such matters; and nothing we'll say will require any sharp line between druthers and dispositions. Where we are not neutral is this point: both dispositions and druthers contribute to personality, and for God to have a personality is for God to have sufficiently many of such.

There are, of course, more dispositions or kinds of dispositions than the ones we gesture at above – one can find them by consulting empirical research in psychology. A quick look at the rest of the "Big Five" inventory as discussed in contemporary psychology, for example, suggests that in addition to introversion we might add specifications of openness to experience, conscientiousness, agreeableness, or neuroticism to our list. And the Big Five is by no means the only theoretical framework on offer.

What is the relationship between these *traits* – particular dispositions and druthers of this kind – and a personality full stop? As follows: to have a personality is to enjoy, to a sufficient degree, sufficiently many of these sorts of traits. How much is enough is not a question we'll broach. A collection of traits may be thought of as a personality profile. From here on out, we will reserve the term "trait" for personality-relevant properties of this kind – druthers, introversion, nostalgia, communication style, sense of humor, and so on. We will use "feature," "property," "attribute," and similar terms more generally to denote any way that God is or might be. Every trait is an attribute (or feature, or property), but not vice versa.

In sum: our central topic is the question of whether God has a personality, which amounts to the question of whether God has enough traits – peculiar aesthetic sensibilities, introversion, or even singular druthers regarding particular people. The hypothesis of divine personality offers an affirmative answer to that question: God is indeed endowed with such personality. Specifications of that hypothesis will say which traits in particular God enjoys.

1.4 Why the Questions Matter

Why should we care whether God has a personality? Are there broader consequences of the view or its denial? Beyond any intrinsic interest, how does it matter whether God has a personality?

First, reflection on divine personality will uncover new angles of approach to traditional wide debates in philosophical theology, such as perfect being theology and the principle of sufficient reason. For anyone who finds those disputes stale, new angles are useful. We may ask, for example, whether or how a divine personality might reflect God's perfection – or whether it is compatible with, or requires revisions to, the principle of sufficient reason. We'll reveal connections, too, between divine personality and traditional philosophical arguments for the existence of God. Theism, say many, is a hypothesis that issues in predictions. Which predictions it makes will vary significantly given the precise specification of theism – and a God with peculiar dispositions and druthers would certainly count as a specification.

Second, we will show connections between a *personalitied* conception of God and some more well-known and narrow topics in the metaphysics and philosophy of religion, including explanation, divine perfection, theological method, divine simplicity, hiddenness, prayer, and more. Exploring a conception of God endowed with personality, we'll show, is fruitful and raises as many problems as it resolves.

Third, a growing cadre of theists depart from "classical theism" and affirm alternative views in the direction of "theistic personalism."[4] Classical theists, we're told, exhibit deep commitment to the absolute simplicity of God, whereas theistic personalists are more flexible on that count, and countenance a God who is metaphysically rather more like the rest of us – perhaps endowed with parts, perhaps a person, and perhaps even subject to the whims of passion.[5] The present study will illuminate the internal coherence of such departures, their consequences, and some considerations for and against. If our arguments are correct, furthermore, the division here isn't nearly so clean as its proponents imagine, and can be replaced or supplemented. Though a God with personality coheres well with the general picture defended by theistic personalists, we'll also show that it can be sustained within a rigorous classical framework committed to, for example, absolute divine simplicity.

Finally, a significant group of theists expresses interest in what they call a personal relationship with God. Indeed, some think that a personal relationship lies at the very heart of piety and joy, and indeed religious life at all. They will assure their cab drivers that God wants to have a personal relationship with them and ask people they meet at the county fair, "Have you entered into a personal relationship with our Lord and Savior Jesus Christ?" Such people have special reason to care about whether God has a personality – and if so, what that personality might be like. To have a personal relationship with someone else is, in part, to become acquainted with their personality – or so it seems. And that acquaintance will show up in various ways, including an enriched and concrete vocabulary when speaking about them.[6] Why should God be any different? An intriguing question, and although our study will not

---

[4] Davies (2004, pp. 2–15). See also Bailey (2021, Section 4), Burns (2015), and Kvanvig (2022).
[5] Mullins (2020).
[6] So Willard (1997, pp. 64–65): "We cannot . . . believe a blank or a blur, much less act on it. There is no 'what' for our minds and lives to lay hold of in such a case . . . To trust in God, we need a rich and accurate way of thinking and speaking about him."

decisively answer it, we hope to provide illumination and points for further reflection, study, and even practical spiritual engagement. One question we'll explore, in the fullness of time, is whether encountering who God is, and knowing God's personality, only involves such obviously "religious" activities as prayer or worship, or might also be aptly pursued in knowing the world God has made.

1.5 Picture Thinking

An image or two may be useful in understanding the hypothesis of divine personality and its import. We propose these images as a supplement to, but not a full replacement of, our exposition of the hypothesis of divine personality.

Consider an empty circle. This one in Figure 1, for example.

Our circle is simple, clean, symmetrical, and orderly. It is defined by just two elements: a radius and an epicenter. From these two, the rest follows. It is homogenous, and without internal structure or character. Its top half is just like its bottom half (but rotated), and so also for any other halves you might identify. And it obeys all of the usual rules that circles obey concerning area, circumference, and so on. It is a tidy geometrical figure.

Now consider a tree trunk, adorned with bark. A picture might help; see Figure 2.[7]

The bark is complicated, messy, and asymmetrical. Whatever order it displays is rather more like that of a fractal than our circle. It has texture and character; it is heterogenous in color, shape, and smell. It cannot be summed up in a simple equation, and it contains mysteries for those who look close. Colonies of fungus may lie in the cracks, and underneath the crusty exterior lies green and living tissue.

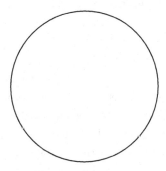

Figure 1 A circle

---

[7] Wikimedia Commons: https://commons.wikimedia.org/wiki/File:Terminalia_tomentosa_bark_pattern.jpg.

Figure 2 Tree bark

We might even say that the strip of bark has some personality. It's got character. It's fascinating. You could spend an hour – maybe a lifetime – staring at the bark and learning ever more about the details to be found within.

With that in mind, perhaps you can already see how these images suggest an imperfect but useful entryway into our topics.

Some people seem to think God is more like the circle than the bark: simple, pristine, without texture or character. But the hypothesis of divine personality suggests the opposite. God is more like the bark than the circle. God is peculiar. God's mind has texture and character. If you could look at it closely and take a sniff, you'd find a cacophony of colors and sounds. God is peculiar and mysterious, with psychological nooks and crannies aplenty.

This is mere picture thinking and subject to all of the usual hedging and caveats that come with such. Picture thinking is no substitute for definitions, analysis, and argument. Of course God is not actually like the bark in these ways. You cannot smell God. The hypothesis of divine personality doesn't say that God has parts, or a fungal colony within, or living tissue inside, or a distinctive tactile profile. And circles can be more interesting than they first seem; π remains a mystery of its own, after all.

That was a visual case. Here's an auditory one.

In your mind's ear, conjure a lone tone sounding at 440 Hz. You could make a tone like this without much effort or expense – your favorite great-uncle's 1981 IBM PC could handle the task without a hitch. No harmonics. No undertones. No timbre at all, really. Just a tone: simple, clean, and pure. One could be forgiven for finding it a bit boring. If you were in a room with the tone sounding out for long enough, you might even cease to notice that it was there.

Now conjure an orchestra tuning up. An oboe begins. As with our tone above, the sound rings at 440 Hz. But this is no mere tone; it's a note – clear and true. If you listened carefully you'd find details within, and all the signs of breath and the lungs that made it. Others follow. The sum result is kind of awesome. And you couldn't make this sound without some pretty fancy equipment – a bunch of bassoons and timpanis and piccolos and so on, and people to play them all. Loads of harmonics. Bathed in undertones. Filled with all kinds of timbre and texture. This is what happens when wood and reed and string and skin vibrate in unison. The result is far from boring, even to a seasoned concert-goer – and even when no symphony follows.

Which one is God more like – the tone or the tuning? On the hypothesis of divine personality, it's the latter. God is not boring. God is fascinating, and overflowing with harmonics and weirdness. If God's mind is a sound, that sound isn't one tone played on a lone instrument; it's the 1812 Overture (cannon edition), or a crescendo from Celine Dion herself.

It is common enough for believers to suppose that God is far beyond our ken and even to use images in making that point. One might say, for example, that God is a vast and dark ocean along whose surface we merely skip rocks. Divine personality fits well within such images. All we need to add is that the ocean is teeming with life; under its waves are funny-looking or scary fish and phyto-plankton aplenty, and perhaps even active volcanoes.

Again, this is all just picture thinking (or sound thinking), and subject to death by endless qualification, if you look too close. God doesn't vibrate. God is not saline.

And yet for all that we find the pictures and sounds helpful in getting a feel for the hypothesis of divine personality. On that hypothesis, God's mind is textured. God's psychology is *interesting* and perhaps even surprising.

God is a total character.

Conversations about the topics of this study, in our experience, unfold in two ways. Some find the hypothesis of divine personality obviously correct: "Of *course* God is a total character – not unlike my favorite great-uncle. God isn't some clean abstract principle. God is complicated and interesting, and far more so than any symphony or tree. Have you not read the Torah? Have you spent an hour in prayerful communion with the living God? Have you looked around you at the playful and weird world God chose to make?"

Others find the hypothesis obviously wrong, or even impudent: "Of *course* God doesn't have a personality. God is absolutely simple, and therefore free of complication, psychological or otherwise. Are you saying God is another slob like one of us? How could a God like *that* be perfect or partless or pure act or serenely unchanging or without potency? Have you not read St. Thomas? Do you remember the warnings of Maimonides? Have you thought for a minute about God as pure Being and no mere being among beings?"

In fact we have. And yet we still have ideas and questions and suggestions we wish to explore. Imagine that.

As you may have guessed by now, our view is a bit more measured than either of these extreme reactions. None of this is obvious. Thinking about God is hard. The evidence is murky. And our own cognitive limitations and biases impede genuine discovery and lead us astray. But progress is possible. One way to realize progress is to construct an initial catalog of considerations for and against the hypothesis of divine personality. We think that on balance, the evidence neither establishes nor refutes the view; instead, it supports a stance of openness to the hypothesis of divine personality. Showing as much is one main task of the sections to come. Along the way, we'll also come to better understand the hypothesis and the problems it prompts.

1.6 Preview

Here is how the rest of this study will unfold.

We begin by removing abstract objections to the hypothesis of divine personality, and as follows: In Section 2, we consider the objection that the divine personality hypothesis makes God all too much like us. For the traits in view are imperfections, or fail to properly contribute to perfection as a well-behaved divine attribute must. We respond that a God with a personality is a character, for sure. Taste and see – THE LORD is weird. But a weird God can also be the God of Abrahamic monotheism, and the God of the philosophers. We reconcile perfect rationality with robust personality, in Section 3, by showing how God's traits can and should figure into the explanation of all other things, and that positing them is not in conflict with the conviction that everything can be explained. We argue, in Section 4, that the divine personality hypothesis is consistent with the views that God is without parts and does not change. Indeed, we suggest that the divine personality hypothesis can aid the proponent of divine simplicity in articulating and defending her own views. Even the most strict and demanding of classical theists may affirm the meaningfulness and truth of divine personality.

Then we switch gears. In Sections 5 and 6, we show how the divine personality hypothesis connects to arguments for and against the existence of God. God may have traits, we say, that enhance certain responses to the argument from evil and the argument from hiddenness, and God's traits themselves may serve as responses to an argument from unanswered prayer. God's traits may furthermore support premises in several lesser-known arguments for the existence of God, like the argument from play and enjoyment, the fine-tuning argument, the argument from order and beauty and structure, and the Mozart argument. We trace, finally, paths from theism to the hypothesis of divine personality. God's own perfection may require a creative personality, even if not any creative personality in particular.

We conclude in Section 7 with a meditation on the limits of our study and how they are to be overcome. Armchair philosophy, unaided by tradition or scripture or experience, can take us only so far. But one needn't stop there, and we provide a case study of how deeper inquiry into divine personality might take form within a particular tradition, and a suggestion that science – study of the cosmos – can itself bring us into acquaintance with a strange and untamed God.

2 The Familiarity Problem

2.1 One of Us

The hypothesis of divine personality is puzzling a few times over. Some, as we've already said, will think it obvious and in need of neither explanation nor defense. But for many others, it will seem hopelessly obscure, a hypothesis in need of expansion. Some will find it impiously anthropomorphic: a disreputable view, and maybe dangerous, whether for the health of one's theology or the eternal state of one's soul. And it will strike yet others as deeply at odds with God's maximal excellence. The problem here isn't just that personality makes God one of us. It's that it renders God less than totally perfect or worthy of all our devotion. If you're thinking about any of these highly general objections to the hypothesis of divine personality, the next few sections are for you.

We can give initial expression to these hunches and seemings using four clusters of hostile rhetorical questions:

- How could we preserve the vital distinction between creation and creator, if the creator turns out to have foibles and druthers and quirks not unlike our own? Isn't that suggestion just making God in our own image?
- How could a God be maximally perfect, while having those foibles and such? Wouldn't these be flaws, or blemishes, or marks against God's supreme excellence? And even if such traits aren't imperfections, they aren't exactly perfections either – so how could we say that a maximally perfect God, a being defined in terms of perfections, has them?
- How could God have *this* personality rather than *that* one? What account could there be of God preferring purple, or having some special affinity toward sons of Abraham? Could such preferences or traits be properly explained?
- Isn't the suggestion that God is psychologically complicated or endowed with rich mental character just the view that God has, in some sense,

internal complexity? And is not that view itself at odds with the doctrine of divine simplicity? How can the God of classical theism be endowed with personality?

These are good questions. They give voice to apparent tensions between the hypothesis of divine personality and widespread convictions about who and what God is – separate, perfect, rational, and absolutely simple. They point, accordingly, to four broad charges anyone sympathetic to divine personality would do well to address: naughty anthropomorphism, opposition to perfection, opposition to reasonability, and opposition to the doctrine of divine simplicity. The charges share a structure: each begins with a conviction in some specification of divine excellence and adds to it a suspicion that excellence of this kind rules out personality. Better to side with excellence than personality, goes the charge; so much the worse for divine personality.

One easy way out is to deny the convictions – to deny that God is, after all, so very separate, perfect, reasonable, or simple. Without those doctrines in place, anything goes – or at least, many things go. Another way out is to weaken the convictions: to ease up on what it takes to be separate, perfect, rational, or simple. Perhaps, this strategy suggests, God isn't so separate or perfect or rational or simple, after all. It may be that one of these obvious ways out is the way to go for the proponent of divine personality. But as we'll see, there are often more interesting routes. It's time to map out a few of them and see where they lead.

Our goal will be largely defensive – not to establish the credentials of the hypothesis of divine personality, but rather to remove barriers to openness to it, especially those that derive from suspicion that a God with personality is just one of us. Later sections will suggest uses for that open stance and possible ways forward for those who adopt it.

2.2 All Too Human

Recall our first cluster of hostile rhetorical questions:

- How could we preserve the vital distinction between creation and creator, if the creator turns out to have foibles and druthers and quirks not unlike our own? Isn't that suggestion just making God in our own image?

Let's think these through.

Many of us – maybe all – are, in our druthers and dispositions, unique or even odd. If you're skeptical, we recommend this exercise: get to know a new person – someone you've never been close with before. Our guess is that the closer you get, the more idiosyncrasies you'll find. People are actually quite interesting – and it's not a stretch to say that they are interesting at least in part because they are blessed with distinctive and interesting personalities. All to the good. Interesting friends, weird friends – they make life better. Interesting people, weird people – they make the world better. We have personalities, and it is good that we do.

It is one thing to praise weirdness in human beings in general and in theory. That's easy. It is another to tolerate it in actual practice. This can be quite hard. And it is yet another to say that God is weird in those ways too. This can be very hard. What if God has some personality traits that we don't like in human persons? What if God's personality turns out to be quite similar to that of your high school bully (minus the morally bad parts)?

Of course there is an obvious and very plain sense in which, compared to us, God must be weird – supernatural, uncanny, out of the ordinary. God is a mighty spirit, the maker of the cosmos, and its supreme ruler. These traits already set God apart from the rest of us. And so it's for good reason that they say that God's ways are not our ways. But to say that God is weird in this context is to say that God is also weird in the ways that we are weird – like a stranger on a bus who seems to have very different musical tastes than your own. To say God is weird in this sense is to say God is one of us. We have personalities. So does God. Our minds are quirky and textured. So is God's. God is, like each of us, a weirdo. A weirdo who is the almighty creator of the cosmos, eternal, benevolent, and so on – but a weirdo nonetheless.

Some readers will balk at the preceding paragraphs for this reason: they are grossly anthropomorphic. The charge is not just that attributing quirkiness or texture to God's mind is incorrect. It is that such attributions are incorrect for a very specific reason: they are incorrect because they inaptly suggest that God is far too much like us. And this suggestion is erroneous or even impious. It posits a God in our own image – all too human, all too familiar.

A most strident version of this objection says that God is wholly separate and unlike us in absolutely every respect. There are no attributes that we share, and no categories under which we both fall. To be sure, the same words can be correctly said of God and one of us. "God is intelligent" is just as true as "Einstein is intelligent." But despite similarity in wording, these two sentences attribute different properties to God and to old Albert, or attribute them in different ways. God's intelligence is not Einstein's intelligence. They're not even on the same scale. And, goes the objection, anyone who suggests that Einstein's intelligence is in any way comparable to God's intelligence, furthermore, is guilty of anthropomorphism. She has inaptly and impiously made a god in her own image – or rather, in Einstein's.

These considerations are fully general. And so they would apply, not just to wisdom or intelligence, but also to personality traits such as introversion, or risk-seeking, or having a favorite color. On this view, God is wholly unlike us, and so couldn't be introverted, or risk-seeking, or disposed toward a favorite color, or given to other peculiar druthers, in any of the millions of ways that we might be.

Proponents of this strident doctrine of separation have their work cut out for them. They must say, for example, how all the sentences we might wish to say about God could be true and meaningful and useful in doctrine and worship and faithful life, despite the fact that their meaning differs wildly from very similar sentences that involve things other than God (intelligence-attributing sentences involving Einstein, for example).[8] This is a familiar challenge. It is just the old challenge of squaring the so-called "equivocal" or "analogical" approaches to theological predication with the apparent meaningfulness and importance of all sorts of sentences about God that appear very similar to sentences about other things.[9] It is unclear, for example, that we have any clue what it means to say God is good, if "good" there means something very different, or applies in a very different way, than it does in sentences like "pleasure is good." Finding and defending good explanations of our predications of attributes to God takes serious work.

But let us, in a fit of generosity, suppose that this work has been done. Let us suppose that a rigid separation between God and everyone else is in place, and that this separation does not do damage to or forbid or render meaningless the sentences we might wish to use in worship or theology or philosophy – sentences like "God is good" or "God is just" or "God is faithful" or even "God believes all truths, and it is true that chocolate is delightful, and so God believes that chocolate is delightful." With this work done, many things may be correctly and piously said of God without any hint of anthropomorphism. All we need to add is that they are to be understood equivocally or analogically.

With all this work in place, the hypothesis that God has a personality is safe from the strident version of the charge of anthropomorphism. For whatever the equivocal or analogical theorist says about other sentences, we may say them about sentences that attribute personality traits to God. In the hands of this strident objector, sentences like "God's favorite color is Pantone 323" may well be true; her theory of theological predication, at least, gives no reason to deny that it. To be sure, the feature attributed to God (or the way in which it is attributed) would not be the same as what's attributed to Kelly (or the way in which it is attributed) in "Kelly's favorite color is Pantone 323." But the

---

[8] As in Keller (2018).   [9] Alston (1993).

sentence about God might still be true. Similar moves would apply to other traits. And so there is no special threat to the hypothesis of divine personality from this strident approach to theological predication.

There is another – less strident, and more interesting – way to formulate the charge of anthropomorphism. Perhaps the problem isn't that attributions of personality traits to God are wrong or that they violate a strict creator-creature divide, but rather that inferences to them are flawed. Overtly or covertly, the idea goes, inferring that God has some personality trait involves making God in our own image – concluding that since we are such-and-so, God is too.

What's to say about this version of the charge? Our first reply is easy. We will not, in what follows, make any overt inference of the form "humans are like this, therefore God is too"; nor will we even argue "humans are like this, therefore God probably is too." If anthropomorphism of the bad variety consists in bad inferences from the human case to the divine, we will studiously avoid it by avoiding any such inferences at all – even the good ones.

We thus avoid the overt version of the charge. What of the covert one, according to which anthropomorphism of the bad variety hides within *any* inference to the hypothesis of divine personality? Here things are more subtle; such is the way with covert operations. The idea may be this: any suggestion that God is like us must at least implicitly involve an inappropriate inferential maneuver. Whether knowingly or not, if you pick some trait human beings tend to have, and attribute it to God, and say God is like us in that respect, then you have moved in the incorrect direction, from human to divine.

We needn't explore the details of the objection to give a high-level reply to it. For it gets things exactly backwards. The proper way to conceive of the view that God has a personality is not that God is like one of us. Rather, we are like God.

Reframing things this way is more than a rhetorical trick. For the reframing – God is not like us; we are like God – points to a deeper reality. The deeper reality is this: human beings are made in God's image. If there is an explanation for why we have personalities, and God has a personality too, that explanation proceeds from God to us. We have personalities because God does, and not the other way around.

This is what it means to say that we are like God, rather than saying that God is like us. Reality is asymmetrical in this sense: if there is an explanation here, God is the explainer, and we are the explained. And it is good and right and pious to insist that explanation runs in this direction. For doing so puts God in a position of priority. This is what piety requires: when things can be ultimately explained, use God, somehow, to do so.[10] Where there is an order of being, God

---

[10] Murphy (2011, Introduction).

is first, and then there's everything else. Of course one must be careful when applying this principle; and there may be notable exceptions to it (some might wish to use us, rather than God, to explain suffering, for example). But it is a good principle nonetheless, and worth at least trying to respect.

What does this observation about the correct direction of explanation say about inferences from our nature to God's? Not much, we think. For – and this is a familiar point – it is often the case that sound and useful inferences run opposite the direction of correct explanation. You can correctly infer that it is raining by observing a wet sidewalk, for example, even though the sidewalk is wet because it is raining (and not the other way around). And the inference here is not just correct; it is one that creates knowledge. The wet sidewalk can evince rain, even to the point of knowledge, even though it is the rain that explains the sidewalk.

Here's the payoff. Even if there were some covert inference at play in the arguments to come, and even if it ran from humans to God, that would not violate pious strictures against anthropomorphic reasoning. For such strictures are best conceived, not as bans on inferences of a particular sort (from us to God), but rather as bans on explanations of a particular sort (from us to God). And we will not resort to the bad kind of explanation.

2.3 What Perfection Requires

We have torn down one kind of barrier to thinking that we share personality traits with God. But there are others. Recall our second cluster of hostile rhetorical questions:

- How could a God be maximally perfect, while having those foibles and such? Wouldn't these be flaws, or blemishes, or marks against God's supreme excellence? And even if such traits aren't imperfections, they aren't exactly perfections either – so how could we say that a maximally perfect God, a being defined in terms of perfections, has them?

They're provocative questions. Let's see what kind of arguments they inspire.

God is maximally perfect. On this Abrahamic monotheists agree. What such perfection amounts to, and which attributes follow from it, are open questions. Some attributes are relatively easy. God is omniscient, knowing anything that can be known. God is omnipotent, able to do anything that can be done. God is morally perfect, holy, wise, and so on. All of these are part and parcel with God's perfection. Because God is perfect, furthermore, God cannot be vicious, cruel, wrathful, lustful, and so on. Unsurprisingly, few have argued that God has attributes such as these, and we may quickly dismiss any version of the divine personality hypothesis committed to God's having such vicious traits.

Those are easy cases. There are harder ones. Is it better to be creative than to lack creativity? Is it better to be eternal than to begin to exist or cease to exist? Must these attributes follow from God's perfection? Or are they perhaps precluded by it? Answers are not obviously forthcoming from pure cogitation on the concept of perfection alone. And there are considerable difficulties with any reasoning at all about God's perfection, and what follows from it.[11]

But many, despite those difficulties, will come to the conclusion that divine perfection rules out personality traits of the sort that are central to this study. One kind of argument here begins with the thought that the traits in view are imperfections. Another concedes that, though the traits aren't imperfections – they wouldn't make God *bad*, or even somehow lacking – but they aren't perfections either.

2.3.1 Traits Are Imperfections

We have already conceded that, if a personality trait is a vice or otherwise negatively morally valenced, God cannot have it. So let us dispatch once and for all any specification of the hypothesis of divine personality involving alcoholism, sloth, greed, envy, and so on. And if time bias is irrational or otherwise bad, God does not suffer from it either.[12] If these are personality traits, they're not the kind God could have, and we may safely set them aside.

Same sample traits we've given involve preferring one thing over another. You might think these preferences require scarcity, and that they concern what their haver would choose or want to do with limited resources. But an almighty God doesn't face this kind of scarcity; for God could, one thinks, simply make more resources. But there are other kinds of scarcity, as when various options are incompatible (making this very item green all over or making it blue all over, for example – it can't be both). And one can have an unmanifested preference too, as when one *would* have selected chocolate over vanilla even though one happily was able to have them both. For these reasons, then, we think sense can be made of divine preferences without impugning God's omnipotence, and we are unconvinced that they are reserved only for finite or imperfect beings such as ourselves. Preferences aren't imperfections, nor do they require such.

Now, our own personality traits can be pluripotent in this way: sometimes they are good, and sometimes they are bad. Your own introversion might lead you toward wise conduct in some situations, but foolishness in others, for example. God's introversion, if God is introverted, couldn't be like this. It

---

[11] Speaks (2018).   [12] Sullivan (2019).

would only be introversion in its most perfected form – never mistaken, never foolish, never excessive or defective, but always present in just the right way, at the right time, and so on. So also for traits of other kinds – druthers, peculiar styles of communication, playfulness, and all the rest.

One might reply that the ordinary cases of druthers, playfulness, introversion, and all the rest are not like this. They are all unperfected, because the people who have them are imperfect human beings. But it would be anthropomorphism, and therefore very improper, to conclude from this observation that divine traits must be similarly unperfected. Let us not be tempted by that suggestion, and turn instead to the question of whether, if perfected, divine personality traits might remain interesting and worthy of exploration.

Take a trait – a specific form of playfulness, let's say – and perfect it. Remove all excess and deficiency from the mix. Those with this trait are inclined to play neither too much nor too little. Add that it is enjoyed in just the right way, and at the right time, and so on. This play never interferes with keeping promises, and is never cruel. Could the resulting trait still be actual playfulness, and recognizable as such? Is there anything left? Or is the resulting trait too thin and gossamer to be worthy of our interest or study?[13]

We think so. We suspect, that is, that something of significance remains after perfection, for playfulness and at least a great many of the candidate traits. And we hope this is the case too, because we think it's better than the alternative. Here's why. Take your own case. Suppose that you have been perfected, maybe after a lengthy process of purgation and preparation for an afterlife of joy. Could your own distinctive form of playfulness remain, or your introversion, or must no recognizable strand of either be left? Could you still be *yourself* – not identical to yourself, but *who you are* – despite being perfected? We certainly hope so. Becoming your best self, as one must do to enter paradise, does not require that you become someone else. It is no part of being perfect that you not be who you are. If this hopeful thought is correct, then there is no obvious war here between distinctive personality traits and perfection of the kind we are to enjoy before entering paradise. And this gives us good evidence that there is no inconsistency between distinctive personality traits and perfection of the kind God has.

It does not strictly follow from this that maximal perfection – God's perfection – is compatible with such traits. But we have dismantled the more obvious reasons to doubt that compatibility, and so we think a stance of openness to that hypothesis is warranted here. That is enough to proceed with our study.

---

[13] Mander (1997, p. 407).

2.3.2 Traits Aren't Perfections

Another style of objection to personality from perfection takes this broad shape: God is a maximally perfect being blessed with all perfections. This is what God is. This is, moreover, who God is. Nothing in who God is falls short of perfection, and everything in who God is contributes to God's perfection. Personality traits – elements within who God is – must also be perfections. But, the idea goes, neither having a personality, nor having a particular personality, nor having a particular trait, is a perfection. And so God doesn't have any of these features. The problem here isn't exactly that the traits in view would make God imperfect; it's that they wouldn't contribute to God's perfection or be perfections, and so are verboten.

There are three arguments here; let's take them in turn.

The first argument has it that God's having any personality at all is inconsistent with divine perfection. Since God is perfect, then if God has a personality, having a personality must be better than not having a personality. But having a personality isn't better than not having a personality. And so, God must not have a personality.

A natural response is that it *is* better to have a personality than to not have a personality. But we shouldn't so quickly dismiss the argument. If it's better to have a personality than to not have a personality, then surely the objectors would have realized that and accepted the divine personality hypothesis. Perhaps the natural response isn't sensitive to the way we're using "personality" in this essay, or is too focused on our own case. Let's think about ourselves for a second.

Is it good that *you* have a personality? We're glad you do. It makes you more interesting. But is being interesting *good*? That would be a substantive claim, and obviously plenty of interesting things are bad, like a serial killer's motivations. So, in general, does something's being interesting count in favor of it? It seems to us that it very much depends on the thing. For a football game, being interesting is good. For a novel, being interesting is good. But for an electrical system? For a law? In some cases, the more interesting a thing is, the worse it is at being that thing.

For a person, being interesting is usually good. And personalities make us more interesting. So, for us, it's good that we have personalities. Some personalities are better not to have, of course; but particular personalities are the topic of the next argument. Overall, people are better with personalities. At least, human persons are. But we shouldn't conclude that, just because it's good for us to have a personality, it's good for God to have a personality. God may (or may not) be a person, much less a human person. And being a good divine being is a very different thing from being a good human person.

The question at hand is whether, for a divine being, it's better to have a personality. Perhaps that question's answer is unknowable. If so, all the better for us. We're investigating whether God might have a personality, and if so, the implications for various other topics in the philosophy of religion. We are not asserting that God does have a personality. And we are certainly not asserting that it's better for God to have a personality than to lack it. It is the objector who's making the claim here, that God does not have a personality because God is perfect and it's better for God not to have a personality than to have it. We do not presume to know that the opposite is true; we are merely suggesting that it might be and thinking through the implications.

If we were to try to determine whether it's better for a divine being to have a personality, we'd begin by looking at other perfections, and asking whether a being that had those attributes would be better off also having a personality. Consider, then, an omniscient, omnipotent, morally perfect, holy, wise (and so on) being. And then consider whether it's better for that being to have a personality. Obviously we're holding fixed the perfections, so having a personality won't impinge on the perfections. Some might think that's impossible, but it's not clear why. Does having a favorite color undermine wisdom? Is it *unwise* to prefer blue to orange? Is it *unholy* to be an introvert? Is it *imprudent* to be quite open to risk? In order for this argument to work, for every personality trait (or collection of such traits, sufficient in number and degree) it must conflict with divine perfection. If that's the case, we'd like to see an argument.

But there's another perfection-based argument that God can't have a personality. This argument doesn't say that having any trait is inconsistent with divine perfection, but rather that divine perfection is inconsistent with God having any particular personality.

God is perfect, says perfect being theology. If God is perfect, then if God has a personality, God's personality must be the best personality. After all, it can't be inconsistent with perfect being theology for God to have the particular personality that God has; we can't accept that God is perfect except for this one particular trait that God has. But there is no best personality. Traits – filtering out the vices and other negatively valenced ones, of course – are just the sorts of things that are neither better to have or not to have, and so many personalities are equally good and vary only according to traits. Or perhaps various good personalities are incommensurable.[14] Or perhaps various very good personalities are not equally tied for goodness, nor incommensurable in that respect, but rather on a par.[15] This, too, would

---

[14] Chang (1997).   [15] Chang (2002).

be a scenario without a best personality. But if there's no best personality, then God can't have the best personality. And if God can't have the best personality, then God can't have a personality at all.

We grant that there is no best personality. If there were a best personality, of course God would have to have it. But if there were a best personality, then its various constituent traits, in that peculiar combination, would be optimal. There'd be a best favorite color and number and football team and place and natural rock formation, there'd be a best risk attitude and a best sense of humor and a best level of comfort in large crowds – or an optimal combination of all of these. But traits of the kinds we're interested in are just the sort of thing that aren't *morally* valenced. Of course, if it's morally better to have some trait than not, then God would have that trait, and if it's morally better not to have some trait than to have it, God wouldn't have it.

One question of this study, of course, is what it would mean for God to have some traits that don't follow from divine perfection. Removing barriers to accepting that idea or objections to it, as we've been doing, is one step toward seeing actual sense in it. The given examples help to further explicate the notion of a divine trait that doesn't follow from divine perfection. You aren't morally better or worse in being extroverted, or enjoying pinkish sunsets over purple ones, or in seeking out risk. You are not in these respects, that is, better or worse than someone without them, nor better or worse than some idealized version of yourself. Your best self enjoys those sunsets too. The point of these examples is not to reason from the human case to the divine one – we are like this, so God is too. It is, rather, to illustrate the sense in thinking of a trait as being neither required by perfection nor detracting from it. Traits of this kind add character, but do not make those who have them morally better or worse.

But maybe there are other meanings of "best" that aren't moral. Maybe there's an aesthetically best favorite color and natural feature and football team, a most mathematically interesting favorite number, a most environmentally important natural rock formation, a most resilient and adaptable risk attitude, a most personable sense of humor, and a most adaptable level of comfort in large crowds. Maybe God must have each of these, or a uniquely optimal combination of them.

That may be. But these nonmoral senses of "best" may conflict with each other. For example, the most environmentally friendly football team – a team that never charters a plane and tries to drive when possible rather than fly and buys carbon offsets and the like – is likely not the most aesthetically pleasing. The most personable sense of humor may not be the most adaptable, and the most adaptable color may not be the most aesthetically pleasing. Moral considerations win out over all these others, but it's difficult to rank them against each other. And since we can't rank them against each other, when they conflict, we cannot determine which God's perfection would prioritize. Indeed, they're just the sorts of priorities that would come from traits.

So, we suspect there's no best personality. Does that entail that God can't have a personality at all? We don't think so. Divine perfection requires that God not have an imperfect personality. Divine perfection requires that there is no personality that is better than God's. Divine perfection does not require that there is one best personality. We can affirm that God has a personality and that God's personality is not imperfect and that there is no better personality than God's personality without affirming that God has the one single best personality. And this is precisely because many traits are not the sorts of things that admit of moral evaluation.

This thought introduces the final argument that perfection precludes personality. It again begins with the thought that God is perfect; thus, if God has a personality trait, it's better to have that personality trait than to lack it. But, as we have repeatedly pointed out, traits of the sort in view here aren't the sorts of things that are better to have, or better not to have. So, God must not have any traits.

Our response is similar to the previous one. Divine perfection requires that God not have any imperfections, and so God may not have any morally bad traits. God can't find it funny when people are harmed without good reason, or prefer shoes made by children for no pay to shoes made by well-paid adults, or the careless destruction of the environment over good stewardship. But it does not require that when traits are morally neutral, God not have them.

One reason for thinking that God cannot have morally neutral traits is that they'd be a distraction. God should actualize the best world, or a really good world if there's no best world. God's sole focus should be on the morally good, then, and making sure it happens. But if God is a fan of Everton Football Club, then God may be distracted by that in carrying out the good. And if God has thousands of traits that are not morally valenced, they will pull God in multiple directions, all away from the good.

This makes sense, when thinking about human persons. Sometimes our traits interfere with our moral duties, such as when we wake up at 5am to watch soccer and then are a tired parent for the rest of the day, or when we purchase a very nice bottle of scotch instead of donating that money to charity, or when we retreat from the family due to introversion at a time when they need our presence.

But we think that divine perfection solves this problem. If God is omniscient and omnipotent and morally perfect, then God would know when acting upon a trait is outweighed by a moral consideration, and God would be able to properly weigh the two considerations, and God would want to do the morally best thing rather than act upon the trait. The things that tempt and foil human plans are no problem for a perfect being. When our own personalities lead us astray, it is due in part to our own finitude and the scarcity of time and power and resources under which we act. But God is not limited in those ways, and so needn't be led astray by introversion or a favorite color.

2.3.3 Optionality

Before turning to more objections to the hypothesis of divine personality, it will be useful to tie together and situate what we've already said within a broader idea that we'll call *optionality*. Optionality says of a domain that it contains distinct, incompatible, and nonetheless equally right or good options.

Optionality is by no means obvious, whether in that highly abstract formulation, or when specified to a more local domain. But it has found proponents and applications. In moral philosophy: in some situations, there are equally good courses of action, and though one may be morally bound to do one of them, no one of them in particular is required. The idea also applies, not just to particular actions, but to programs for action; here some find room for variation and moral style.[16] In epistemology: for some bodies of evidence there are distinct permissible, excusable, or even justified propositional attitudes one might take toward a target proposition: strong belief, middling belief, withholding judgment, and so on.[17] In aesthetics, as when there are distinct, incompatible, but equally effective ways of pursuing some creative or artistic goal (we'll say more about these kinds of cases, below). What these versions of optionality have in common is a resistance to sweeping uniqueness requirements on what is good or right. Those stern requirements simply demand too much.[18]

Optionality is one natural and well-furnished home for the hypothesis of divine personality. There is no best way to be, when it comes to introversion or extroversion. There is no ideal stance toward risk. There is no best favorite color. Nor is there any best combination of any of these traits, or any others; there is no best personality profile, that is. There isn't even an unending and ascending scale of personality profiles, each better than the last. The idea of a best personality simply doesn't make sense. These denials cohere well with the broader view that personality is a domain subject to optionality. Though some options in this domain may be better than others – see our discussion, above, about vices or imperfections – there are nonetheless elements in it that are distinct, incompatible, and equally right or good. Defenses of optionality in other domains, furthermore, may prove to be fruitful to defenders of divine

---

[16] Axinn (1990). [17] Schoenfield (2014), *contra* Horowitz (2019). [18] Woolard (2016).

personality. If stern uniqueness requirements fail elsewhere, they may well fail here, and thus make logical room for a God who is maximally perfect – as good as can be – and who also enjoys optional features not required by that perfection.

Optionality suggests one final reply to the objection that, since any given trait or profile isn't a perfection or required by maximal perfection, God can't have it. The reply is this: though a given trait or personality profile isn't strictly required by perfection, it is one of several whose disjunction is so required. It is better to enjoy that disjunction than not, and God enjoys that disjunction by way of one of its disjuncts. So the trait or profile is, in a way, a perfection. For it is a particular way in which God is perfect.

There's another potential reason for thinking that in cases of genuinely neutral traits, God cannot have them. If God has a trait, that fact is explained; and the only kind of explanation that will do is that the target trait is better to have than some salient alternative. But such explanations are not forthcoming for traits that are neutral in the target sense. And so God hasn't got any.

This is a valid argument, and it will be compelling to many. But we think it's mistaken. To see why, we'll need to more thoroughly consider explanation and its demands. That is the topic of the next section.

3 The Problem of Perfect Rationality

3.1 A Reason for Everything

It is time to work through our third cluster of hostile rhetorical questions:

- How could God have *this* personality rather than *that* one? What account could there be of God preferring purple, or having some special affinity toward sons of Abraham? Could such preferences or traits be properly explained?

We propose to transform these questions into arguments by deploying a venerable old idea known as the Principle of Sufficient Reason. In its most potent form, it says that, without exception, everything must have a reason or explanation why it is so rather than not. Professor Walker drank kopi gau this morning, and so there's an explanation of why he drank kopi gau rather than not. And it's not just choices or even contingent truths that require explanation. Three is prime, and so according to this Principle there is some explanation why three is prime rather than not.

As you might guess, the Principle stated in such strong terms finds resistance. And so its more accommodating proponents dilute its content. One such dilution restricts its scope only to what is contingent – what could have been otherwise. Another demands, not a full contrastive explanation – why something is so *rather than* not – but only an explanation why it is so.[19]

And from this Principle or its diluted variations, we may derive a few general objections to the divine personality hypothesis. In broad form, all of them say that God's personality either in whole or in part would be *inexplicable* and thus beyond the pale. We simply can't make sense of the idea that God's personality or its constituent traits are explained; and so they are not, and so it must be the case that God has no personality.

In fact, this style of objection doesn't require something as grand as the general Principle of Sufficient Reason, potent, or otherwise. It could be levied from a formulation restricted just to God. So where the Principle of Sufficient Reason begins with the conviction that everything must be explicable, the Principle of Divine Reason (as we might call it) says more modestly that everything about God is explicable.

Why would one accept the Principle of Divine Reason but not the Principle of Sufficient Reason? Here's one idea: some portions of the cosmos are subject to randomness or chance or simple brute fact. A subatomic particle swerves here, or decays there, for no reason at all. But God isn't like that. Who knows what electrons get up to in their free time or when we're not peeking – perhaps there is no full accounting for what they are or what they do. But, at least in principle, a full accounting could be given for every element of God's being and behavior.

Why would God be especially explicable in this way? One answer links reason with perfection. Inexplicability is an imperfection; things that are explainable are better, more complete, or more perfect in some important respect than those that aren't. And so God, being perfect, is explicable. Another answer derives from optimism about theology, whether philosophical or otherwise: to inquire in a field is to presuppose that there are answers to our questions within it.[20] And answers to questions are or involve explanations. So if theology – the study of God – is a proper field of inquiry, God's being and behavior are explicable. If God has a trait, there is an account of why. And so we may expect, if God has personality traits, that they can be explained. We might not know the explanation, but there is one.

Consider now, in Table 1, some possible formulations of the Principle of Divine Reason, each a restricted formulation of the Principle of Sufficient Reason.

Each of these principles will furnish an objection to one or more formulations of the hypothesis of divine personality.

---

[19] Pruss (2006, p. 10; pp. 148–155).   [20] Amijee (2022a).

Table 1 Principles of sufficient reason

	Restricted	**Unrestricted**
Contrastive	Every contingent fact about God has an explanation of why it is so rather than not.	Every fact about God has an explanation of why it is so rather than not.
Not contrastive	Every contingent fact about God has an explanation of why it is so.	Every fact about God has an explanation of why it is so.

3.2 From Reason to No Personality

It is time to fill in a few details. We envision an objection with two broad steps.

The first step says that if God has a personality, then it or each of its constituent traits must have an explanation. This step derives from the Principle of Sufficient Reason, or from one of the specifications of the Principle of Divine Reason noted in the grid above. Since there is variation between those specifications of the Principle, there will be various ways to develop this first step. If the target divine personality hypothesis is one according to which God's personality holds with necessity, then an unrestricted version of the Principle will be required to unseat it. A contingent variation of the hypothesis of divine personality, by contrast, would be vulnerable to both restricted and unrestricted principles.

A more complicated form of step one might say that each of God's constituent traits must have an explanation in terms of some other traits, or some particular trait – that they all come as a package deal, as it were, with explanatory links holding the package together.

The general idea behind step one is not mysterious. It stems from stolid resistance to mystery and a conviction that mystery of a certain sort is impossible. Not even God is beyond this strict ban on mystery, according to step one; and so God's being and behavior are themselves explainable. It doesn't follow from this that we'd be able to understand the relevant explanation, of course. But there would be one. For every fact about God, including facts about God's personality, there'd be some account of why it is so – and maybe even why it is so rather than something else being so, if a contrastive version of the Principle is being deployed. When it comes to God's alleged personality traits, we may always ask "why?". And there must always be an answer.

The second step adds that there simply couldn't be an explanation of God's personality or its constituent traits. Try as we might, the idea goes, and you'll not find an account of why God is introverted, or given to nostalgia, or prone to reserved – or grandiloquent – styles of communication, or drawn to people whose names begin with "J."

This second step could be especially impressive if a contrastive requirement on explanation is in view – if a contrastive version of the Principle is used to generate the first step, that is, since we'd need the same requirement to show up in step two for the resulting argument to be formally valid. For it is hard indeed to see how there could be a contrastive explanation of, for example, God's attraction to people whose names begin with "J" rather than those whose names begin with "K," or rather than having no such attraction at all. One letter is as good as any other, one thinks. In any case, this second step concludes, we can't find the relevant kind of explanation. Contrastive or not, it eludes our search. The fact that we cannot find an explanation for them suggests that there isn't one. And so, on reflection, and given the dearth of forthcoming explanations such traits would have to be unexplained or brute.

If the personality traits in view were consequences of perfection – if God's maximal perfection required a deep aversion to risk, for example, or if some other familiar divine attribute plainly entailed that God had scarlet as a favorite color – then this second step would face trouble. There would be an explanation of God's having these traits. And indeed, it would be simple to state: God has them because they are a consequence of maximal perfection, or omniscience, or some other familiar divine attribute. But we are most interested, in this study, with traits that are not obvious consequences of perfection or any other familiar divine attribute. But if God's maximal perfection, or goodness or knowledge or power or whatever, did not explain why God's favorite color is scarlet, what else could? No answers seem forthcoming. And so the second step commands significant initial plausibility.

Putting these steps together, it follows that God has no personality.

The objection here resembles a kind of argument that is common enough elsewhere in philosophical theology: if God were like *that*, the idea goes, some element of God's being or character would be pure happenstance – metaphysically mysterious and inexplicable – and thus right out.[21]

It's a formidable challenge. And we concede that there's something to it. It does seem that personality traits of the sort in view are too arbitrary and contingent and optional to attribute to the Almighty, even if we enjoy them ourselves. It's not just that they'd tell against God's moral perfection, though they might do that (see Section 2.3). It's that they'd tell against God's reasonableness or logical nature or coherence or something of that sort. God is pure

---

[21] Rea (2016, pp. 106–107).

logos with no hint of *chaos*; and so God couldn't have some wildly inexplicable trait, nestled within the other familiar and orderly divine attributes.

3.3 Three Replies

There is much to say about this broad style of objection. We could issue picky complaints about the details. But we think all objections of this kind suffer from significant defects at a much higher level. And no version of the Principle of Divine Reason furnishes us with a strong reason to reject the hypothesis of divine personality.

3.3.1 Modesty

Our first reply takes a page from the skeptical theist's book. Skeptical theists offer a family of replies to atheological arguments from evil that exploit our own cognitive limitations. We can't be confident about our own ability to spot and understand the various kinds of goods or evil there might be, or connections between them, says the skeptical theist.[22] And so we cannot confidently conclude that there aren't good reasons for God to permit the latter. What might otherwise appear to be strong evidence against the existence of God is, when evaluated in the light of our own cognitive finitude, significantly less impressive. Our finitude here poses all sorts of trouble, and not just for atheological arguments.[23]

A similar maneuver applies here. Suppose that divine personality traits are inscrutable in this sense: we simply cannot conceive of how they could be explained, especially in terms of God's other traits. To conclude from this that there are such explanations is to make a noseeum inference: "I don't see 'um, so they ain't there."

Now, some noseeum inferences are plainly good and right. When you look for a bottle of water on your otherwise empty but well-illuminated desk and see no bottle, you may be forgiven for concluding that there is no bottle. But when the lights are off, or when you're not sure you can even remember what your water bottle looks like – not so fast. Your own cognitive limitations, or the limitations imposed by your environment, are a blockade against any quick and easy noseeum inference here. And if you can't find the light switch, or get better information about your water bottle, there may be no way around it.

We see a similar blockade here. The mere fact that we don't see how something can be explained isn't, as such, a strong reason to think that it is indeed inexplicable. The faster you move, the slower you age. Time dilation of this sort may have appeared inexplicable before 1905 – and indeed may still appear inexplicable to

---

[22] Bergmann (2001).   [23] Hudson (2014).

many. And yet it is not inexplicable. The laws of nature – the constancy of the speed of light among them – explain why time dilation happens.

There's an important lesson here: our initial bafflement at a phenomenon isn't decisive evidence that there isn't a way to make sense of it all. The bafflement may say more about us than the phenomenon. We are finite creatures, and when things get too complicated, or beyond our imaginative powers, or when biases cloud our minds, there is good reason to doubt whether we'd be in a position to spot explanations, even when they're present.

And when it comes to God's own mind and personality, things are complicated and beyond our imaginative powers, and biases arise that cloud the mind. These cognitive limitations give us strong reason to doubt whether we'd be likely to conceive of the correct explanation of God's personality or some trait within it *even if* there is such an explanation.[24] There's reason to think that we're ill-equipped for that task.

And so, the simple fact that we can conceive of no explanation for a divine personality or trait is no good reason to conclude that they are indeed inexplicable.

Much of what we've said thus far should appear familiar – not because it borrows from skeptical theism, but because it borrows from what proponents of the Principle of Sufficient Reason must say when defending their favored principle. Some things appear unexplained. Appearances are misleading, say those proponents; and this is just what to expect for creatures like us. There are hidden variables in nature, and our inability to spot them is no evidence they're not there. So also, we say, for nature's creator.

Proponents of the Principle of Sufficient Reason have also attempted to show that there could be contrastive explanations of God's free choice to create – without specifying what those explanations might be.[25] We'll not comment on whether those attempts succeed. But if they do, they bolster the modesty pressed here and its openness toward the idea that there could be explanations about which we know very little.

We have thus far interpreted step two as an inference. It could, of course, be a flat assertion that there just couldn't be an account of the relevant kind (contrastive or not) for God's personality or its constituent traits. That would do the trick, in terms of sustaining a valid argument. But is it credible? We think not. We think that reflection on the cognitive limitations highlighted above gives us reason to be agnostic about such assertions, in fact. This stance is even more sensible for a proponent of the Principle of Sufficient Reason, who already countenances a plethora of explanations for all things, the details of which are hidden from our plain view.

---

[24] Howard-Snyder (1996, pp. 299–300).   [25] Pruss (2016).

3.3.2 Exception

Our second reply targets step one. It goes like this: precisely because of God's role as an ultimate explainer, we have good reason to think that the Principle of Sufficient Reason does not apply to God. Appeal to the Principle of Divine Reason gets things exactly backwards, in fact. It's not that there's special reason to think God's being and behavior are explained; rather, there's special reason to think God's being and behavior are unexplained.

Explanations are the rule. God is the exception.

Here's why. Abrahamic monotheists find God behind all things. Ask "why" enough times – here it may be helpful to recruit the help of a curious five year old – and you'll encounter an explanation that involves God. Why can't we watch any more gorilla videos? Because the laptop is out of battery juice. Why does your laptop behave the way it does? Because electrons do such-and-such. Why do electrons do such-and-such? Because the laws of nature are thus-and-so. Why are the laws of nature thus-and-so? Because God made them that way. Because God. And once you've reached God, there's little else to say.

God is the unexplained explainer. And God is unexplained, for this reason: if God's being or behavior were explained, there would be either something else behind God, some more ultimate reality, or there would be a vicious circle or regress of explanations within God. The first option sounds blasphemous; nothing outside God lies behind or explains or is prior to God's being or behavior. The second and third options sound goofy. Explanations can't go round in circles or recede forever. Not everyone thinks this, of course, but theists tend to. And indeed this is sometimes why they are theists; they think that, since explanations can't go round in circles or recede forever, there must be a God. And so, for anyone inclined to posit God as an ultimate explainer, there is a good reason to think that God is unexplained.

Some theists might balk, and insist that in their view, God's attributes are indeed explained – by God's perfection, or some other core property, say. To see whether the move makes sense, we need only ask of God's perfection whether *it* is explained. Sure, God is perfect. But *why*? We suspect there is no answer here, and this is precisely why God's perfection is thought to be a good core from which to extract the rest of the divine attributes. But this concession – that some of God's attributes are indeed unexplained – should make us wonder why personality traits, or some other attributes that explain them – couldn't themselves be unexplained too.

Our reply will find ready allies from those who insist, on grounds of divine simplicity, that God is beyond explanation. On this view, God is so simple as to transcend the distinction between objects and their properties; in divine Being, there is no such distinction at all.[26] And so one cannot sensibly look for or find reasons why God has this property or that. We'll say more in Section 4 why proponents of this radical version of divine simplicity can still affirm divine personality; what matters here is that they have resources to resist an objection from explanatory requirements.

Thus, our second reply. We do not say this reply is decisive, of course, but we think there's much to recommend it – especially to the theist. Step one errs in that it expects God, of all things, to be explained. But the theist should think this expectation is erroneous, and so the objection to divine personality fails.

3.3.3 No Reason

Our third reply also targets step one. And unlike our second reply which derived from the ultimate explanatory role God is often thought to enjoy, the third derives from a wholly secular – and for many philosophers, entirely familiar – objection to the Principle of Sufficient Reason. We will therefore be mercifully brief on this point.

The big idea is this: the Principle of Sufficient Reason implies that every truth is necessarily true, itself as implausible a consequence as any.[27] And so the Principle must go. Here's the argument for that broad idea: if there are contingent truths, then there is a conjunction of all of them. According to the Principle, there is an explanation of this conjunction. But what could explain it? Not one of its conjuncts; that would be a thing explaining itself. So its explanation must lie in some other truths, and necessary truths are the only candidates that remain. But proponents of the Principle think that explanations strictly entail what they explain – note its use of "Sufficient." So, the necessary truths that strictly entail the conjunction of all contingent truths must strictly entail that conjunction. And every truth entailed by a necessary truth is itself necessary. So the conjunction of all contingent truths is itself necessary. Contrary to appearance, things could not have gone otherwise than they actually do if the Principle of Sufficient Reason is true. Since the consequence here is so implausible, the thing to do is just to reject the Principle that got us there.

Is this an iron-clad attack on the Principle of Sufficient Reason? Of course not. It faces objections at every turn. And so we present the argument, not as a decisive conversation-ender, but with full knowledge that some will accept its premises. If you're of that mind, then you have a reason to doubt this style of objection to the divine personality hypothesis. And if not, there's always the other two replies given above.

---

[26] On that alleged distinction, see Rettler and Bailey (2023, Section 1.2).

[27] van Inwagen (2015, pp. 164–167).

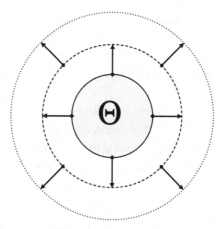

Figure 3 Divine choice, divine personality, and explanation

3.4 Personality and Explanation

We have argued that there is no good objection to the hypothesis of divine personality from general considerations about explanations and its demands. We could end things there. But it will be useful to say a bit about the role that personality can play in explanations that appeal to God, and see what follows.

We'll begin with a picture. Behold, Figure 3.

Before talking about the Theta in the middle (spoiler: it's God), let's work through some other elements in the chart. The outer dotted circle represents the cosmos in all its contingent glory. Here we find electrons and planets and people and elephants and all the contingent truths about them. Working inwards, the dashed circle represents God's choices. And the arrows between these two represent explanation. God's choices explain the contingent cosmos. Behind the electrons and trees and planets and people and elephants we find divine decrees – God's choices about what to create, what laws are to govern those creatures, and so on.

What explains God's choices? Maybe nothing. One could decline to answer the question, on the grounds that they are unexplained altogether. A better answer, we think, appeals to God's nature. What explains God's choices is *what* God is.

And so we come to the inner sanctum, the aforementioned Theta, and the explanatory heart of all things – or, at any rate, of all things that can be explained. Here we find, not what God does, but what God *is*. The facts here are not idle, when it comes to the outer circles. For God makes various choices, such as selecting broad ends to pursue, and the means to pursue them, because God is a certain kind of being – perfectly good and just, say.

Must we only appeal to what God is when explaining God's choices, though? Must *what* God is be the only item within that inner circle? We think not. We think it useful – and quite natural, really – to appeal here to *who* God is. And thinking of things in this way promises an enriched explanatory role for God to play.

A revised chart will illustrate; where there was once a Theta, let there now be what – and who – God is. These, together, lie at the explanatory heart of all things, as in Figure 4.

And though we've used a plural term here – "these" – that plurality shouldn't be taken too seriously. The suggestion is not that there are two items, *who God is* and *what God is*, which two items together play a certain explanatory role. To commit to such plurality would put us at risk of denying divine simplicity (on which more, in Section 4). A better and more simplicity-friendly interpretation might deny that phrases like "who God is" denote anything at all, or concede that they denote, but deny that their denotations are in any sense proper parts of God, or perhaps concede that they denote, but insist that both "who God is" and "what God is" denote nothing less than the Almighty. So though the revised chart has two words in its center, in reality there's just one Theta.

Supplementing the inner circle in this way promises an enriched explanation for God's choices.

What are God's ends? And how does God select the means by which to pursue them? These are good questions, and on the model at hand they are to be answered by appealing to who and what God is. God's ends are those selected by perfection. And where there are multiple pathways to those ends, perhaps tied for perfection or incommensurable in that respect, God's personality fills the explanatory gap. It is here that we most naturally appeal to who God is.

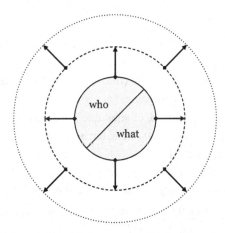

Figure 4 Divine choice, divine personality, and explanation, again

God's perfection selects the ends – or some of them, at least – but the journey along the way, the *style* in which they are pursued, these are selected by God's other traits.

Look closer at the chart, and you'll see two kinds of arrows. Some have boxes at one end, and some have diamonds. Both kinds of arrows represent explanations of some sort or another. But we may wish to deploy different styles of explanation; hence, two kinds of arrows. When God decrees that something be so, it is so. It must be. From an outright order that there be light, it follows that there is light. The light is explained, furthermore, by the order. The explanation in view, there, is entailing. What is explained is entailed – logically required – by its explanation. Could there be explanations, however, that lack this logical strength, that explain without entailing? Perhaps so. And perhaps this is the kind of explanation that links the inner circle – who and what God is – to God's choices. God's choices are indeed explained by this enriched inner circle, which includes both absolute perfection and a personality consistent with it – but nonetheless not entailed. That's one way to go, at least. It will appeal, above all, to theologians who insist that God's choices are free, and that free choice requires various genuine possibilities.

These charts leave many questions unanswered, and you can probably already think of alternative charts worth drawing and contemplating. Terrific. Please do so.

But in the meantime, we draw a lesson. The hypothesis of divine personality is a useful – theoretically fruitful – doctrine. It fits well with, can supplement and expand on things theists already say about God and the explanation of all other things. Which fruit it bears depends on the details and on which configuration of the hypothesis is in view; and there are many such configurations.

What are these configurations, exactly? We can illuminate many by raising a few questions:

- Must God have a personality? (must there be a "who" as well as a "what" in the inner circle?)
- Must God have *this* personality? (must the contents of the "who" be fixed, or could they have been otherwise?)
- Is God's personality prior to, or subsequent to, God's choices? (could the "who" belong, not in the inner circle, but as an intermediate circle between the dotted and dashed circles?)
- Is God's personality explained at all? (do we need all those arrows?)
- Is God's personality explained by other standard divine attributes, or in some other way? (what kinds of arrows are we to draw in the chart, and in which direction should they run?)

One may here mix and match. You might think, for example, that God must have some personality or other, but no personality in particular. God's traits would be contingent determinates of a necessary determinable, in that case.[28] You might think that certain of God's traits are subsequent to God's choices – that God chooses, in part, who to be – and that subsequent choices about what to create are explained by those elements of who God is. And so on.

Here's why we raise these choice points and possibilities. Commitments elsewhere in metaphysics or theology will impose constraints on what shape a theory of divine personality must take. And yet there are options here. Lots of them. In many cases, we can respect an important constraint in one domain by fiddling with variables elsewhere. Before concluding that the divine personality hypothesis is to be rejected, it would do philosopher well, we think, to look at the menu of options, to try on various charts for size, and to thus find out whether some variation might in fact fit well with other cherished convictions.

4 The Simple Problem

4.1 God without Parts

There's just one more cluster of hostile rhetorical questions to address:

- Isn't the suggestion that God is psychologically complicated or endowed with rich mental character just the view that God has, in some sense, internal complexity? And is not that view itself at odds with the doctrine of divine simplicity? How can the God of classical theism be endowed with personality?

Here is the broad idea: we know, whether by Scripture or tradition or pure reason, that God is absolute without parts (taken to include any distinctions, potentialities, or divisions) of any kind.[29] But if God has a personality, then God has parts of some kind or other. So much the worse for divine personality.

We have much to say about divine simplicity that we won't say in the present study because it's irrelevant. We're interested not in whether God is absolutely simple, but whether God can be absolutely simple and have a personality. We think that the answer is yes.

Proponents of divine simplicity tend to agree that God is omniscient and omnipotent. They must then give an accounting of God's omniscience and omnipotence that is consistent with divine simplicity. If Maimonides is right, "Those who believe that God is One, and that He has many attributes, declare

---

[28] Wilson (2023).

[29] For penetrating discussion of just how strong this doctrine might be, see Ward (2020, Section 5).

the unity with their lips, and assume a plurality in their thoughts." We'll display more charity, and grant that they do have an answer. We suggest that they simply apply that answer to divine personality traits.

They might balk. Perhaps they think a personality makes God too complicated – more complicated than the traditional divine attributes that they're used to explaining. By way of reply, we note that things may *look* to us more complicated than they actually are. The proponent of divine simplicity thinks of God like a single unbroken segment. But even a single unbroken segment may appear to us in incredibly complicated ways.[30]

Another objection to the reconciliation of divine simplicity and divine personality is that traits don't look like each other, or like standard divine attributes. Justice and mercy and love and knowledge can, when you squint, sort of look like each other. But those aren't the only divine attributes. If God is simple, then God's love is God's power. God's knowledge is God's wrath. It takes quite a bit of work to show these identity claims.

In fact, we think that appeal to peculiar traits could *help* defend these identity claims. For example, God's justice doesn't look much like God's mercy. Justice demands retribution and punishment, while mercy demands forgiveness and compassion. Or so it seems. But add this trait: risk-aversion.[31] If God is risk-averse, then divine justice tempered by risk-aversion may sometimes require retribution and punishment, and other times forgiveness and compassion. The more general lesson is this: with the right personality traits in hand, divine attributes that seemed superficially diverse may enjoy deep unity. The proponent of divine simplicity may thus find divine personality to be an ally, not an enemy. And given what she says elsewhere about divine justice (that appearances notwithstanding, it is identical to divine goodness, to divine power, and indeed to God), she is hardly in a position to complain that, appearances of diversity must be given special weight here.

4.2 God without Change

A related objection lurks nearby. God is perfect. Any change in God would require that either God is no longer perfect, or that God was not perfect – neither option is viable. Similarly, change requires internal complexity, something from which God is entirely free. Thus, and twice over, God is without change. But if God has a personality, then God changes. So, God must not have a personality.

---

[30] See the mazes at http://mrszotos.weebly.com/assignment-2-maze.html, each created using a single unbroken segment.

[31] Buchak (2013, pp. 13–36).

This objection to divine personality proceeds from the doctrine of divine immutability, the view that God does not change. There are various ways of making this more precise. One way is to claim that God is faithful in keeping promises, or that God's character remains the same. Another way is to claim that none of God's intrinsic properties change, although God can undergo changes in relation to other beings because those beings undergo intrinsic change. The final and strongest way is to understand divine immutability as the claim that God is wholly unchanging in any respect at all. There are a mighty host of objections to the strongest version of divine immutability – hence the existence of the weaker versions – but our purpose in this study is not to evaluate the principles or argue against them, but to show their connection to the divine personality hypothesis – even if the connection is that the principle in question entails the denial of the divine personality hypothesis.

However, none of the three versions of divine immutability entail the denial of the divine personality hypothesis.

Consider the weakest reading first: God is unchanging with respect to character and promises. God doesn't value things differently over time, God doesn't break promises, and so on. On this way of understanding divine immutability, it doesn't entail that God lacks a personality.

Nothing about having a personality requires a change in traits. So, an easy response to the charge that the divine personality hypothesis violates divine immutability is that God's traits never change, and thus God never changes. Divine immutability is preserved in letter and in spirit.

This reply rules out some of the example traits we've been thinking through. God has a favorite football team, suppose – but club football has only been around since the 1800s. Did God have a different favorite sport prior to the invention of football? Did God adopt a football team in the 1800s and stick with them through thick and thin – and the introduction of thousands more football teams? Did God have a favorite color before the creation of the world and carry on with it until today? Perhaps. But perhaps not.

Suppose that God's traits do change. After 100,000 years, God begins to prefer green over blue. God becomes more introverted as the human population grows. God's first favorite football club was the Edinburgh Foot-Ball Club, but when Everton was founded in 1878 God began supporting them. God started off risk-seeking, but became increasingly more risk-averse as human suffering expanded in power and scope. Would these scenarios violate this weakest reading of divine immutability? No obviously so. For they don't, as stated, require breaking promises or anything like that – just as a spouse may remain faithful despite shifting culinary preferences.

The second specification of divine immutability says that none of God's intrinsic properties change, although God can undergo changes in extrinsic relation to other beings. Intrinsic properties are the ones that a being can have when alone, whereas relations require at least one other thing. God can be omnipotent, eternal, good, wise, holy, just, and necessary without any other being existing. These are intrinsic properties. But God cannot be creator, sustainer, judge, redeemer, protector, provider, or healer in a world with no other beings than God – there being no one around to redeem, judge, and so on; at most, God could intrinsically be these things in potency only – disposed to redeem, to administer justice, and so on.

We doubt the proponent of divine immutability would affirm that God can change with respect to being creator, sustainer, judge, redeemer, protector, provider, or healer. These are not the reason for weakening the divine immutability thesis to only concern intrinsic properties. Instead, the reasons for doing so have to do with properties like favoring Abraham above all others, speaking to Samuel in the night, passing over the houses with lamb's blood on the doors, and such. Each of those are extrinsic relations God bears to things in the world, and that come and go over time.

So, the question relevant to this understanding of divine immutability is whether the divine personality hypothesis entails that some of God's intrinsic properties change over time. Suppose, as we've already suggested, that traits aren't elements of God's nature – they are no part of *what* God is. But are they *intrinsic* properties nonetheless? Answers here will vary by trait. God is an Everton supporter; this requires Everton to exist and so is an extrinsic relation. God prefers the color blue over green. If colors aren't somehow within God, this too is an extrinsic relation (otherwise, not).[32] But God's being risk-seeking requires nothing else to exist, and so may be intrinsic. God can be introverted whether or not any other people actually exist, and so introversion seems intrinsic – in worlds where God is alone, it may still be true that *were other people to exist*, God would prefer solitude.

All that the divine personality hypothesis requires is that God has sufficiently many of the relevant properties from Section 1. It doesn't require any particular ones, or any particular kinds. Many on the list appear to be extrinsic relations, and God could have a very interesting personality just by combining some extrinsic ones. Given the wide variety of options, it's entirely plausible that God has only extrinsic properties of those kinds and has sufficiently many of them to a sufficient degree so as to have a personality. So, the divine personality hypothesis is consistent with this reading of the divine immutability view.

---

[32] Ward (2020).

Two down, one to go.

The strongest version of divine immutability says that God is wholly unchanging in any respect at all. Every property God has, God has at all times. God never gains any properties, and God never loses any properties. Any relation that God stands in, God stands in at all times. Unlike the times, God is ne'er a-changin'.

Even this strong formulation of divine immutability is compatible with the divine personality hypothesis. Our personalities change over time, as we learn and grow and experience new delights and horrors. God needn't be like that, though. And certainly those who are initially drawn to divine immutability would have reason to think that God's personality doesn't change. Any trait that God has is stable.

So, all three versions of divine immutability are consistent with the divine personality hypothesis. Some versions allow God to have more traits than others, but each allows God to have sufficiently many traits to a sufficient degree as to constitute a personality. No barrier to personality from immutability.

4.3 Personality Outside the Box

We have one more reply to the objection from divine simplicity. The objection in its most basic form unfolds in two moves. First: God has no parts. God has no structure. God has no divisions within. Second: to posit a divine personality is to posit internal structure, or complexity, or parts, or division. And so God is without personality.

Let's look at that second move a little more closely.

It is certainly tempting. We've said that God's personality answers the question, not of what God is, but *who* God is. And it is certainly tempting to think of who someone is as a matter of things going on inside her – of involving internal structure, complexity, parts or division, that is.

But this temptation may be resisted. Here is an alternative to consider in its stead.

Many personality traits are extrinsic and relational. They are outwards-looking, world-involving, and present only in the company of others. Perhaps you know what this is like: some element of who you are that is deeply tied to another beloved (or loathed) person, or a place, or a social setting. It's not just that these people, or places, or settings occasionally activate a trait that is already there and fully within you. Rather, the trait itself is bound up with those people, or places, or settings. You cannot say who you are without calling them out by name.

You have heard it said that we are social animals; to say that we enjoy traits like these – extrinsic and relational – and that they nonetheless encode who we are – is one specification of that venerable saying.

Of course, God isn't a social animal. God isn't an animal at all. But that isn't the end of the story here. God might have these extrinsic and relational traits, not of necessity and by nature as we do, but in some other way. Yet reflection on traits as extrinsic and relational remains instructive. For if all of this is correct, we have a general reason to reject the claim that personality traits must involve internal goings-on. Perhaps some do. But many others do not. If there is a ban on internal divine complexity, it would only rule out the former, and not the latter.

And so we have a fully general recipe for resisting any objection from divine simplicity. That doctrine forbids internal complexity in God. But if divine personality traits are to be understood as external, in whatever sense is relevant, it evades the charge altogether. Though divine traits may lie at the explanatory heart of all things – in the inner circle of our charts above – they may nonetheless, at least in part, lie outside of God.

Some have thought that contingent intrinsic features in God face a difficult and intractable explanatory burden: how could God be that way, except by pure happenstance?[33] Those two elements conspire to make the question especially pressing. Since the target feature is contingent, it didn't have to be there. Since it is intrinsic, no explanation outside God may be given. We have argued above that the problem isn't so intractable as it seems; for there is little reason to be confident in our ability to spot explanations, even when they are there. Locating God's personality traits outside the box furnishes one more reply. For traits or profiles, even if contingent, needn't be thought of as intrinsic.

You might suspect that our proposal is outside the box in another and more important sense: outside the bounds of orthodoxy and in conflict with the doctrine of divine aseity, or perhaps that of divine self-sufficiency. For it would seem to entail that who God is depends at least in part on items outside of God. That inference is too quick, though. Imagine that – perhaps after noticing some unusual pyrotechnical activity in nearby flora – you asked the Almighty "Who are you?", and you got this answer: "I am the God of Abraham, Isaac, and Jacob." It's not as though, in saying this, God didn't answer your question (the God of Abraham, Isaac, and Jacob really is who God is); nor is God's answer here at odds with aseity, despite the fact that the answer involves created beings external to God. God couldn't be the God of Abraham without there being such a man as Abraham, after all. But this obvious fact in no way besmirches God's aseity. The lesson is this: it's tempting to hear "who God is" as meaning something like

---
[33] Rea (2016, p. 107).

who God must be or *God's personal nature*, or *who God is, intrinsically*, and so on; but if these are the only permissible interpretations, then "I am the God of Abraham, Isaac, and Jacob" either does not answer the question given, or answers it incorrectly. Neither option is viable. So it's better, we say, to conclude that there are weaker but nonetheless natural interpretations on which "who God is" may denote conditions that involve created beings outside God, all without violence to plain meaning or good doctrine.

We are not the first philosophers to propose that God has a personality. Indeed, Michael Rea beat us to the punch some years ago. Where we suggest that God's personality traits are extrinsic and relational, Rea has suggested that God " . . . has a unique personality that is at least partly expressive of God's own purely *self-regarding* interests and desires."[34] The proposal here thus parts ways with Rea's.

But despite that apparent difference, there are deeper points of concord. So Rea:

> If the writings of contemporary philosophers of religion are any guide, many will be content with a concept of God as somehow less than perfectly personal. Although God is typically characterized as a being with personal attributes – knowledge, love, power, and so on – it is also fairly typical to find God talked about in ways that make sense only on the supposition that God is little more than a kind of machine whose programming requires it to entertain and affirm as many truths as possible while at the same time causing, allowing, or preventing worldly events in such a way as to maximize various kinds of moral and non-moral goods. Of course, nobody explicitly *says* that this is how they think of God; but (so I say, anyway) it is hard to read much contemporary philosophy of religion without getting the sense that this is in fact the picture that underlies much of it.[35]

We share Rea's impressions. We also think that, when philosophers and theologians treat God with such abstraction, it is not for no good reason. There are principles that properly govern thinking about God, and God's maximal perfection is one of them. Any hypothesis at war with that principle is to be rejected. What we have shown, in these preceding sections, is that divine personality is not at war with the principle. We have removed an important class of barriers to accepting the hypothesis.

5 Arguments against God

Divine personality is, we've argued, compatible with some classic and venerable doctrines – that God is separate, perfect, rational, and absolutely simple. We'll now connect the divine personality hypothesis to some classic and

---

[34] Rea (2018, p. 75, emphasis in original).   [35] Rea (2018, p. 75).

venerable arguments – and some newer ones – with an eye toward whether a God with a personality uncovers new problems or solutions for these arguments.

We'll first consider three arguments against the existence of God: from evil, from hiddenness, and from unanswered prayer. We'll use the argument from hiddenness as a focal case study, going into some depth about the argument, extant solutions, and how the divine personality hypothesis relates to the argument and to the extant solutions. Then we'll present the other three arguments and sketch out the connections with divine personality, leaving many details to the reader.

We take this approach because we see something in common in all three arguments – arbitrariness. God prevents some evil, but allows other evil. God provides evidence sufficient for belief to some people, but not others. God answers some prayers of some people, but not all prayers of all people. God saves some and not others. In short, God apparently chooses – which evil to allow, which evidence to provide and to whom, which prayers to answer, and which people to save.

We've argued that if God has a personality, then God's personality can and should play an explanatory role. So, when we encounter puzzles like the ones above, we should look to God's personality for possible resolutions to them.

God makes choices, it seems – and so selects from various possible options. Could God's personality explain why God selects in this way? We think so.

It's a familiar pattern of inference in the human case, after all. Chocolate isn't better than butter pecan, but some people prefer it. Blue isn't a better color than green, but some people like it better. And there's no further fact about those colors in virtue of which the people prefer it. Perhaps they can reach for an explanation – "it's relaxing," "it's the color of the sea," "it's the color of my eyes," or the like – but it's not as though those features guarantee or actually account for the preference. Not everyone prefers their eye color over all other colors. Everyone agrees that blue is the color of the sea (Homer excepted), but many people still prefer other colors. Some may agree that blue is more relaxing than red, yet prefer red because it's more exciting. And when Maya selects blue clothes, it comes as no surprise. For an explanation is ready to hand: Maya chose blue clothes because she prefers blue over green. It's one of her druthers.

We're not saying that, since human beings have traits, God has them too. That would be the forbidden anthropological inference. Rather, we're saying that if God has traits, they will likely play an explanatory role in some of God's choices, just as they do in our own.

5.1 Hiddenness

5.1.1 The Problem

It is good to believe that God exists, if God indeed exists. For one, it's good to have true beliefs. But this belief – the belief that God exists – isn't just any old belief. It's important in a way that the belief that there are seven sheets of paper on this desk isn't important. The belief that God exists has the potential to structure people's lives in a way that few other beliefs do. It affects what you read, who you interact with, where you go, what leisure activities you treasure, and much more.

God, if real, surely knows how important this belief is. God, being omniscient, knows everything, including the importance of theistic belief and all it enables. God, if morally good, loves everyone. And not just the way that people love a fast new iMac, or even a long-time family pet. If God exists, God loves us with the love of beneficence. God wants what's best for us, and pursues our good.

So, we've established the importance of belief that God exists if it's true, and that God knows of that importance and pursues our good. Since it's good for us to believe that God exists (if it's true) and God knows that it's good for us and God wants what's good for us, then God would want us to believe that God exists. This is true of everyone.

But not everyone believes that God exists. And this is not because they are resistant to God. There are a great many people who'd very much like to believe that God exists, yet don't. The evidence hasn't persuaded them. One could say, we suppose, that they secretly are resistant and either haven't admitted it to us or perhaps even to themselves. But it seems implausible to think that is true of every person that lacks the belief that God exists.

God knows that these people don't believe but want to, and also knows how important it is to them to believe. God wants these people to believe. And given God's omnipotence, God could easily provide them sufficient evidence to believe that God exists. A few well-placed miracles, a few visions or dreams, a few answered prayers … trivial for God to do, and there would be far fewer nonbelievers – perhaps even zero.

5.1.2 Replies

So, why doesn't God furnish everyone with evidence sufficient for belief, or faith, or devotion? Some say that God does. But, they say, every nonbeliever is resistant. They don't want to believe in God. Despite having access to plenty of evidence such that their belief in God would be justified were they to believe on the basis of the evidence they have, they fail to believe. That strikes us as pretty implausible because we've met some counterexamples. But we're not evaluating responses here – merely connecting them with divine personality.

If every nonbeliever is resistant, perhaps God doesn't force the evidence even more strongly on people because God is not given to forceful expression. Perhaps expressions of self-focused braggadocio make God uncomfortable – especially if it's something that would be required millions or billions of times. And so God, being more reserved, lets people make their own choices.

Another response to the argument from hiddenness involves free will. Freedom is a great good, the response goes. And any divine plan that could make *everyone* a believer would be disrespectful of the free will God finds so important for us to have.

But why is free will such a great good? Dogs and cats don't have free will, you might think, but we love them anyway and seek out their company and our emotional lives are bound up with theirs. Why couldn't God have been satisfied with our being only nearly free, or free only in the ways that dogs and cats are, but not free with respect to belief in God?

Maybe we can think of an impersonal answer to that question, or an answer that has to do with us. But a useful personality-based answer is also ready to hand. We prefer that our children not act on their free will in certain ways, like hitting or screaming or refusing to go to bed. But all things considered, we prefer that they have real free will, rather than whatever free will a dog has or whatever free will that their toy robots have. We like to spend time with people endowed in this way – not just for their sake, but for ours. It's not just that it's better for there to be such people in some abstract sense – maximizing utility, say. We just like it better. Whatever personality trait accounts for this liking, perhaps God has a relevantly similar one, and it's that trait that explains why people have free will and why there are nonbelievers.

Another response is skeptical theism, which you'll remember from Section 3.3.1. Skeptical theism asserts that we shouldn't be confident about our own ability to spot and understand the various kinds of goods or evil there might be, or connections between them. And so we shouldn't confidently conclude that there aren't good reasons for God to permit nonbelievers – perhaps that permission allows for some goods or avoids some evils in a way we just can't see.

The above extant answers needn't specifically appeal to divine personality, although we've seen that divine personality can offer some further reasons to accept them. But other extant answers appeal more essentially to divine traits.

Personality-based replies to the argument from divine hiddenness (or silence) begin with the suggestion that God's hiddenness is an expression of God's personality.[36] The particular trait of God's personality that explains divine hiddenness could be one of several – introversion, shyness around people one doesn't know very well, aloofness, reservedness, quiet attentiveness, reflectiveness, privateness, the list goes on.

Some of these seem negatively valenced; others do not. Some of the ones that seem negatively valenced likely seem that way because of our own personalities and the way we experience humans who exhibit that trait. Setting aside issues about theological predication – whether "aloof" means the same thing in "God is aloof" and "Murphy is aloof" and whether traits like *being aloof* apply just the same to God and humans – we know that an aloof being who is otherwise perfect will exhibit that aloofness in a very different way than a human person who is aloof and also has some imperfections.

Of course, the reader should feel free to cross items off the list that she considers to be imperfections. But the reasoning of the previous paragraph suggests that we shouldn't be too quick to rule out traits that seem to be imperfections because of our experience with them as exhibited by human persons. We must consider, too, any perfected form they might take.

Suppose God is introverted, then – a trait that's neither a perfection nor an imperfection – and consider how thinking of God as introverted might change our evaluation of the argument from hiddenness. The argument from hiddenness says that if there were a God, there'd be no nonbelievers. What would it take for all the nonbelievers to become believers? What kind of evidence do they require? And how would an introverted God feel about having to provide all that evidence?

It might take a lot of miracles that God could successfully orchestrate from on high. But that still might not be enough. Indeed, it's not obvious that any evidence would be enough.[37] But if there were evidence that would be enough, it might be the evidence of personal interaction. Lennay can send you hundreds of texts and have dozens of phone conversations with you, but the only way to know for sure that she exists is to walk over and meet her for yourself.

That's a very demanding standard for an introverted person to live up to: having a meeting with every person who doesn't believe that you exist and convince them that you do. Of course, God is omnipotent and this isn't an impossibility for God (unless some people are essentially nonbelievers), so God *can* do it. But that doesn't mean God must do it. God's omnipotence doesn't

---

[36] Rea (2011, p. 271).   [37] Rettler (forthcoming).

mean that this is not a very demanding standard for an introverted God. Or a reserved God, a quiet God, a private God. It might be a standard that, if adhered to, would conflict with other elements in the divine personality – an epistemic style, for example – a distinctive approach to evidence and its sources, how it is to be weighed, and so on.[38] A God with preferences in epistemic matters (between competing but equally reasonable options, to be clear) may well have preferences about how others are to come to knowledge of the divine, which sorts of evidence are best to give, and so on.

But we must weigh God's traits against God's perfections. We've argued that God may have traits that are neither perfections nor imperfections, as long as those traits don't conflict with divine perfection. But one might wonder whether a trait can conflict with a perfection *at a particular time*. Many parents are introverts, and there are times that their children demand their attention when they'd rather be left alone. The right thing to do (at least usually) is to pay attention to the children. When people demand God's attention, it seems that even an introverted God should (at least usually) pay attention to the people. But there are billions of people, so God's attention is constantly demanded. It seems reasonable not to expect God to always come running when people call.[39] However, God is omniscient, and one could be forgiven for thinking that God should have thought about that before creating a world that would come to be inhabited by billions of people. We would rightly criticize a parent who adopted several hundred children partly because we would know that the parent couldn't possibly give enough attention to each child. If God wouldn't be able to provide each human person with enough personal attention to bring them to belief in God, then God would have known that in advance and shouldn't have created – so the objection goes.

So, the divine personality hypothesis doesn't decisively settle the argument from hiddenness. There are resources for a response, but they raise new problems. The same goes for other potential personality-based responses to the argument that posit other traits or that posit druthers. It's worth looking at one druther God might have to see if druthers might work as a response.

Druthers, recall, are affections, preferences, or other traits directed at particular creatures. God might prefer the sons and daughters of Abraham, for example, over other people groups. Perhaps that's because of their personalities, or Abraham's personality, or something else – or perhaps there's no further explanation of that druther.

As with more general dispositions like introversion, druthers may play a role in responding to the argument from hiddenness, whether in identifying justifying

---

[38] Flores (2021).   [39] Rea (2018).

reasons or compensating goods for God's allowing nonbelief, or in simply being the justifying reasons or compensating goods themselves: God is hidden because that is a consequence of who God is.

5.2 Evil

God is omniscient, omnipotent, and morally perfect. Being omniscient, God knows everything, including the moral valence of all goings-on – bad, good, neutral. Being omnipotent, God can prevent any evil. And being morally perfect, God wants to prevent any evil, provided that there isn't some compensating good or justifying reason to leave it be. But our world contains unprevented evils, without any compensating goods or justifying reasons. So, our world must not contain an omniscient, omnipotent, and morally perfect being.

This is one classic argument from evil. In its most general form, it contends that any evil at all is inconsistent with the existence of God. In more nuanced forms, it contends that the existence of evil provides evidence against the existence of God. And in some forms, it says of particular evils that they are inconsistent with, or provide evidence against, the existence of God.

One needn't take the argument from evil to show that there is no God, that God is lacking in goodness, power, or knowledge, or anything like that. It might show, rather, that there are some unnoticed and peculiar connections between various possible goods, between goods and evils, and so on. God, being omniscient, can see connections we do not detect. Evils go unprevented and possible goods go unrealized because God is working within constraints we haven't noticed, whether toward compensating goods or in accordance with justifying reasons.

Questions remain. Why did *these* possible goods go unrealized, in favor of *these* compensating goods? Why are *these* justifying reasons in place rather than others? Perfection alone supplies no answers, especially in cases with goods or reasons that are tied. A divine personality can help. If indeed there are justifying reasons or compensating goods, what might explain their status as such is God's valuing them more highly than the instances of suffering they justify or compensate for. For example, God might value empathy more than pain avoidance, and so let people suffer so as to understand others' suffering (think here of God displaying this preference between scenarios that are tied for goodness, so the preference is not simply a result of one being objectively better than the other). God might value spiritual growth over temporary comfort. God might value moral development over a life of pleasure and ease. It's not obvious that these traits entail that human persons suffer, but one can see how traits might play a role in explaining some instances of suffering.

Peculiar druthers can help here too. God might allow Alex to suffer so as to avoid Jade suffering because God prefers Jade to Alex. God might allow Mike to suffer because it will bring about great goods for Matthias and Penelope, and God gets along better with Matthias and Penelope than with Mike.

Divine personality traits may thus play a role in responding to the argument from evil. Whereas in the case of hiddenness we suggested that God's traits may just be the justifying reasons or compensating goods themselves, it is hard to see how they could in the case of the argument from evil. But they may supplement particular justifying reasons or compensating goods, or complete explanations otherwise lacking.

5.3 Prayer

Here's another argument against the existence of God. People pray. Often, they ask for things. This is petitionary prayer, and it raises a number of vexing puzzles.[40] Some people get what they pray for, and some people don't. Sometimes, apparently similar petitionary prayers receive different replies; Mike and Ryan pray for Arsenal to beat Everton, while Brad and Duncan pray for Everton to beat Arsenal – God grants Mike and Ryan's prayer. Hold fixed the goodness (or good-enough-ness), or badness of the request. There will still be apparently arbitrary differences in whether God answers the prayer or doesn't answer the prayer. Two individuals may request the same thing, for the same reason, and in the same circumstances, and yet God might grant one request and not the other; Lori and Marie pray to be cured of their cancer, and God grants Lori's prayer but not Marie's. Since the cases do not relevantly differ, there can be no satisfactory explanation for the pattern of silence and reply. But, many will suppose, there must still be a satisfactory explanation for all that God does (see Section 3).

Put another way: the following four claims are inconsistent: Sometimes there is no relevant (internal) difference between two prayers. If there is no relevant (internal) difference, then God has no reason to give different replies. If God has no reason to give different replies, then there are no cases in which the same cases receive different replies. But there are cases in which the same request receives different replies. The problem gets worse. There are not just pairs of prayers, as it were, that raise unsettling questions about whether God is responding reasonably to prayers. There are no discernible patterns of silence and reply, and so God's answers display little rhyme or reason. One might conclude that there is no God at all, and be done with the mess.

---

[40] Rettler and Parker (2017), Thornton (2023).

As before, appeal to divine personality traits can help. Peculiar druthers concerning those who pray – God just likes Lori, or feels some affinity to Mike – provide the rhyme (or more likely the reason) for some prayers being answered and others not.

6 Arguments for God

The divine personality hypothesis may play a role in bolstering arguments for the existence of God, as it did in bolstering replies to arguments against the existence of God. We begin again with a case study – the argument from play and enjoyment. Then we'll briefly sketch three additional arguments where we think a similar strategy could be employed, leaving the details to the reader.[41] Our claim here is not that these arguments succeed or that they are sound. It is, rather, that they may be cast in a more favorable light when developed in tandem with a hypothesis of divine personality.

6.1 Play

We begin with the argument from play. Human beings derive pleasure from playing. We have fun, we joke around, we laugh. These things make us happy. We didn't have to be this way, and it's not remotely obvious why we are. Perhaps early play and joy prepare us for the future and thus help us pass on our genes. But of course, we players are rare among the fauna. Squirrels, arachnids, and ants do not play, and yet their species flourish. We have a capacity to experience joy that, perhaps unlike rationality, seems unnecessary to our survival.

It isn't obvious that our ability to play and find joy supports the existence of God. A transcendent perfect being – a goodness maximizing machine, as it were – needn't have any interest in our having such capacities. A God like that wouldn't find much humor in hide and seek, a karaoke party, or dogs wearing funny hats. But we do. Even a personal God with all the classical divine attributes wouldn't obviously care about play or joy. Pleasure, sure. Survival, that too. But play? This is harder to see.

So, the fact that we play and have the capacity to enjoy it sets us apart from much of the animal kingdom, and invites explanation. It doesn't seem that evolution can do the job. But a God with personality can.

A God with a personality can find enjoyment in all sorts of things – even surprising things. And a God who finds enjoyment in things would naturally find enjoyment in creating, and in particular, creating beings who also find enjoyment in things. A whimsical God might want lots of variety. An

---

41 The arguments to be discussed in this section come from Plantinga (2007).

extroverted God might want lots of people. A playful God might want lots of fun, and people to play with. And so on.

Now, in this section, we're considering the argument from play. "From" is important here, because we're reasoning from the fact that we play to the existence of God. We've suggested that our playing doesn't give us much evidence for a transcendent perfect being, or even a personal God who lacks a personality. But our playing does evidence a God nonetheless – a God with personality, or at least some of the traits suggested above.

There is a familiar tradeoff in all of this. Theism plus the hypothesis that God has a personality, or particular traits, has a lower prior probability than theism all alone. And yet the resulting argument – the argument from play for a God with personality – might nonetheless get a leg up here, because it offers a more compelling explanation of the target phenomenon than it could if using theism alone. In any case, we recommend that proponents of the argument from play reflect on this variation, and consider whether their argument is most properly construed, not as evidence for theism alone, but as evidence for a peculiar version of theism on which God has a personality.

6.2 Fine-Tuning

The fine-tuning argument for the existence of God commands serious contemporary attention – and rightly so. According to this argument, we get evidence for God from noticing our own existence. Of course, it's a bit more complicated than that. First, we consider some evidence from cosmology regarding the physical constants of our universe. For example, if the force of the Big Bang explosion had differed in strength by 1 part in 10^{60}, the universe would have collapsed back in on itself or expanded too fast for stars to form. If the ratio of proton and neutron masses were slightly different, one would have decayed into the other – and both are needed for life. If gravity had been stronger or weaker by 1 part in 10^{40}, there wouldn't have been stars. The upshot: the range of values the constants could have that allow for organic life is vanishingly small.

Now, the probability that the constants would fall in that narrow range of values that allow for organic life if it were just left up to random chance is as small as the range relative to all the possible values, which may be as small as the range divided by all the numbers – infinitesimal. The constants could have had any values, and the chance of any one set is the same as any other.

But the probability that the constants would fall in that narrow range of values that allow for organic life if God were in charge of setting the constants is not so small. God might have particular reasons for setting the values of the constants in ways that allow for life.

So, given that the probability that the values of the constants would fall in that narrow range is higher given the God hypothesis than the chance hypothesis, the fact that the values of the constants fall in that narrow range is evidence for the God hypothesis over the chance hypothesis.

Some have, for a variety of reasons, objected to the premise that the probability that the constants would fall in that narrow range of values that allow for organic life if it were just left up to random chance is very small. We won't discuss that premise or objections to it, because we don't think it's related to the divine personality hypothesis.

Others have criticized the premise that the probability is not low on the God hypothesis. They've wondered how in the world we can claim to know the mind of God, and assign probabilities to things based on our knowledge of what God would want. The divine personality hypothesis can help us in defending that premise. If the divine personality hypothesis is true, God has traits. God's traits serve as an explainer.

As before, this lowers the prior probability of the God hypothesis, since it adds to that hypothesis. The prior probability of a God with a personality is lower than the probability of a God, since the former is a conjunction that includes the latter. But it makes creation – and, when developed in the right way, creation of the very kind we observe – more likely on the observed evidence.

6.3 Order, Beauty, Structure

A related argument concerns the nature of the natural world. Newton wondered, "Whence arises all this order and beauty and structure?" These are three distinct features of the natural world. The world is ordered: migratory birds fly thousands of miles following a similar pattern annually, the seasons change at predictable times in predictable ways, things are made up of DNA, and so on. The world is beautiful: sunsets change from blue to pink to red to violet, fireflies and jellyfish glow with bioluminescence, and the earth's landscape is as varied as desert and jungle. The world is structured: ice crystals and snowflakes exhibit a hexagonal prism lattice pattern, a beehive's honeycomb maximizes honey storage, pinecones' spiral arrangement protects seeds and maximizes dispersal.

These features of the natural world may not be in need of explanation; perhaps it's all chance and natural selection. But for those who think they are in need of explanation, and that a theistic hypothesis can help, we suggest they supplement their arguments with divine personality. The world displays order and beauty and structure because it was crafted by someone who values order and beauty and structure – and not just any old order and beauty and structure, but the very kinds we observe.

6.4 Mozart

The previous argument talked about beauty – perhaps the natural world contains beauty because God enjoys beauty. A related argument for the existence of God comes from our appreciation and grasp of beauty. Human beings always and for the most part enjoy beauty. We create and participate in and watch dances, we listen to music, we are mesmerized by visual art. And not mainly bad dances and music and art, but good – Anna Pavlova, Bill Robinson, Mozart, Cedar Walton, Basquiat, one could go on. An evolutionary explanation for this appreciation is tempting. But many animals are just as successful at reproducing and thriving without noticing beauty at all – beetles, cockroaches, dogs, and so on. And, one thinks, it could have been the case that humans found beauty in non-beautiful things – garish patterns, cacophonies, and jerky motions – without disastrous evolutionary consequences.

Enter God – or so says the proponent of the Mozart argument. We enjoy Mozart's works, and other beautiful artifacts, because there is a God who made us this way. And why should God have made us this way? Perhaps the explanation for our appreciation of beauty concerns God's personality. Perhaps God recognizes and appreciates beauty, and created human persons to do the same. Perhaps it pleases God to share with us the beauty of creation and the beauty of each other. And perhaps it pleases God for us to be correct in our aesthetic judgments. All of this requires, not that there be a perfect God, but that there be a God who displays aesthetic proclivities and wishes to share them.

Thus a few arguments for theism. Our point, again, is not that these arguments succeed; rather, it is that they may be fruitfully developed, supplemented, and in some cases enhanced, with the hypothesis of divine personality.

What we say about these arguments, furthermore, has wide application elsewhere in natural theology. For the hypothesis of divine personality may provide a useful supplement when answering a standard objection to arguments for theism; and reflection on all of this will help us map out yet other routes that reason from theism to personality. Let's take up both of these ideas, in turn.

6.5 Mind the Gap

Arguments for theism sometimes display a gap.[42] They conclude with the existence of some being, possessed of an admirable quality – that a necessary being exists, that a mighty creator of the cosmos exists, that an all-knowing being exists, that a source of goodness exists, and so on. But why should that being be a god, much less the one true God? Is there any reason to think that the being identified in

---

[42] Oppy (2014).

the conclusion of these arguments has *all* of the admirable qualities, much less maximal perfection? These questions are pressing, and they point to a gap between the official conclusion of an argument and the conclusion its designers hope readers will draw.

Natural theologians have helped themselves to various strategies in bridging the gap. Some find deep unity in the admirable qualities, so evidence for one is evidence for all.[43] Others adopt a more piecemeal approach, moving from one quality to the next, and so gradually piecing together a conclusion that looks increasingly like maximal perfection.[44] And yet others enrich the hypothesis argued for from the beginning and so incur the tradeoffs already noted above. They add additional conjuncts to their target hypothesis – rendering it closer to full theism – and so better explain the evidence at hand, at the expense of that hypothesis' simplicity and prior probability.

The hypothesis of divine personality, we suggest, points toward some fruitful ways of pursuing this third gap-crossing strategy. One could enrich the hypothesis argued for by adding traditional divine attributes, or positing maximal perfection in all its glory. Or one could add something rather more narrow – just one trait, like a predilection for covert over overt communication, say. Would the resulting hypothesis – that there is a being who enjoys necessary existence and a covert communication style, say – be better than alternatives at explaining the relevant data, or in surviving scrutiny of its prior probability? How about other combinations of traits with traditional divine attributes? Are traits really more simple than attributes?

These are fine questions. We won't answer them here. But we recommend reflection on them to anyone interested in pursuing the project of natural theology. We trust that they will bear fruit in the form of both new styles of argument for theism, and new kinds of evidence, for and against.

6.6 From Theism to Personality

So far we've been considering arguments for the existence of God that are strengthened or modulated in interesting ways when supplemented with a hypothesis of divine personality. Let's change tack for a bit, and consider arguments from theism to divine personality. Some of the aforementioned arguments may be made to fit the bill – supposing there is a God, the best explanation for the fact that human beings enjoy play is that God has a personality. Supposing there is a God, the best explanation for the fact that the natural world is beautiful and that human beings perceive and appreciate and seek out that beauty is that God has a personality.

---

[43] Mooney (2019).   [44] O'Connor (2004) and Rasmussen (2009).

6.6.1 Cosmic Winks

There are other features of the world that don't seem to figure in good arguments for the existence of God but do seem to figure in an argument for divine personality on the assumption that there is a God.

Nearly anyone born in the last 50 years is familiar with *Super Mario Bros.*, and knows that the chief villain of that Nintendo franchise has been, since 1983, an anthropomorphic turtle named "Bowser." What some may not know is that the current president of Nintendo is a man named Doug Bowser. That's hilarious. And if there's a God who exercises some degree of providence, it's some bit of evidence that God is (benevolently) mischievous.

Acclaimed scientist Steven Hawking was born on the 300th anniversary of Galileo's death, and died on Einstein's birthday. Edwin Booth, the son of John Wilkes Booth, saved the life of Robert Todd Lincoln – the son of the man his father assassinated. The sun is 400× larger than the moon, but also 400× farther away from us, making them appear the same size and making solar eclipses possible. These are all fascinating coincidences, and if there's a God, provide some evidence that God appreciates a world of homage. Some have argued that our cosmos is fine-tuned for life; perhaps it is fine-tuned, as well, for intrigue or for fun.

6.6.2 Perfect Artistry

Those suggestions were rather specific. But they point toward something far more general than simple nominative determinism or the coincidences that issue from it, or even to the feeling that the universe is winking at us. It is that the cosmos itself can, if you look at it right, display personality. This is evidence that its maker does too.

We have already argued at length that perfection is compatible with personality. Our approach there was defensive – to pry open some space for a curious picture of who God is. But perfection can furnish a positive case for personality too.

We'll explain with an analogy.

Consider a skilled artist – a composer, say. And suppose that her skill has been made manifest; she's actually written a truly great film soundtrack: stirring, replete with emotion and power, finely tuned to the images and words and sounds it accompanies. A soundtrack like this wouldn't be generic. It would, rather, deploy specific techniques – chord voicings, styles of melody and harmony, particular orchestrations, pacing, modulations in amplitude, and so on. It's not that these specific techniques would be the only worthy or even truly great ones to use, given the storytelling and emotive tasks at hand. For here there is room for variety; there isn't exactly one perfect soundtrack to go with a given sequence of film, that is. And yet our composer made choices. She selected some techniques over others. And these selections made her soundtrack have the character it has. Her disposition to select some techniques over others, in a field of equally good options, is in part her musical personality. Though being a skillful composer doesn't demand any musical personality in particular, it does require musical personality. It is never bland or generic in its expression. Great art is done with style.[45]

Maybe perfection is like this. Maybe, when creatively expressed, it requires selection – not between good and bad options (the choice there would be all too obvious for a perfect God), but rather between equally good options. Not poison or water, but chocolate or vanilla. How might God – a perfect creator, one thinks – handle such selection? We could reply that God simply declines to choose; selection between options is random, instead, outsourced to some dice. We could also reply that God chooses them all, and so creates, not one cosmos, but many cosmoi – a multiverse, as they call it. Like the child who grabs both chocolate and vanilla cones, the God of the multiverse has it all.[46] Or we could reply that God, like our composer above, is disposed toward certain techniques over others – chord voicings, colors, timbre, framing and setup devices, and more.

The randomness reply will be unsatisfying for those who think God doesn'tplay with dice, and for anyone attracted to the Principle of Sufficient Reason. It may simply press us into accepting the personality hypothesis anyways – perhaps God selects by rolling dice because God enjoys the trait of being *risk-seeking*, for example. The multiverse reply is interesting. But it, too, may simply map another path to personality. For could not the resulting multiverse, like the long, storied, and diverse portfolio of a productive composer, itself displays patterns that evince creative personality?

We think, in any case, that there's a decent case that God's perfection requires some creative personality or other, though it requires no creative personality in particular. There is thus a path, not to theism, but from it – to the divine personality hypothesis.

And the point extends beyond initial creation and into God's ongoing activities in the cosmos, if such there be – sustaining laws, interaction with creatures, and even the redemption of all things. Others have argued that God's defeat of evil involves a distinctively aesthetic element.[47] Could those aesthetic elements involve genuine artistic choices between equally good options, and where what is at stake in those choices is a matter of pure

---

[45] Ross (2005).   [46] Amijee (2022b, pp. 297–299).   [47] Adams (1999).

style? If so, they are further opportunities for expression of divine creative personality.[48] The opportunities will be no less subject to the usual qualifications and foibles of ordinary inferences from style to personality, one suspects.[49] But they may nonetheless furnish further arguments that proceed from theism to personality.

The suggested path raises as many problems as it solves. For one, what is the explanatory connection, if any, between God's perfection and some creative trait? Here are three broad approaches.

First, we could say that the trait is not explained at all. It's just there. This would incur the wrath of proponents of the Principle of Sufficient Reason, and it is a route we've already touched on, above.

Second, we could say that the trait is explained, and explained by God's perfection, but that the explanation in view is not an entailing one. So, though God's perfection strictly entails that God has a creative personality, it entails no specification of that personality. One consequence of this view is that God's creative personality varies across various possibilities; variation of that sort is just what such contingency means. Some will balk at that consequence. For it holds, not that God could change, but that God could have been endowed with different traits. One extreme interpretation would conclude from such possible variation that God could have been someone else. These are good doubts. But perhaps the doubters may be persuaded. For in a way, the consequence in view – variation of personality across possibilities – makes good sense. No wonder the cosmos looks *this* way over here in modal space, and *that* way, over there – for God, the creator of the cosmos, has a different creative personality across those possibilities. And the most extreme interpretation of this variation can be rejected. God is not *someone else* in these alternative possibilities. Rather, the details in who God is vary.

Third, we could say that God's creative personality is indeed explained, and in an entailing way, but perhaps not by God's maximal perfection alone, or in a way we could possibly understand. Perhaps there are other divine attributes – beyond or aside from those plainly implicated in maximal perfection, that is – that together explain and entail that God has *this* creative personality, goes one version of this idea. Or perhaps God's perfection alone explains and entails this creative personality, but we simply have no way of seeing how either of those connections work.

How plausible are any of these three broad approaches? We've raised a few considerations for and against; but these do not settle the matter. For the correct answer here will turn on, among other things, the necessary shape of

---

[48] Robinson (1984, Section I).   [49] Riggle (2015).

explanation, and the extent to which we should expect to understand the inner workings of God. These are tough topics, and figuring them out is no easy task. There is plenty of work yet to be done.

6.6.3 Heterodoxy

We have emphasized throughout this study the ways in which divine personality fits well within orthodoxy, in both letter and spirit. We have a gift, though, for those willing to stray from the most strict statements of classical theism. For nonstandard forms of theism also generate arguments for the hypothesis of divine personality. Pantheism, for example, identifies God with the cosmos.[50] Does the cosmos display *style* or *character*? Are there patterns we may observe in its constitution and distribution, patterns not predicted by traditional divine attributes alone? Do these patterns indicate peculiar druthers somewhere at play? If so, there is an argument that these patterns do not merely evince divine personality. They *are* divine personality. When the cosmos winks, so to is God. If the cosmos is a total character, then so is God, for they are one and not two. Arguments along these lines will also emerge if the cosmos and its creatures are, as some have supposed, contained within God's mind.[51]

6.6.4 Valuable People – with Style

One more suggestion. People are valuable, and valuable in a special way. We are special in many ways, of course – for unlike many other denizens of the cosmos, we can think and feel. The value we enjoy, furthermore, is non-fungible. You can't replace one of us with a molecule-for-molecule duplicate without loss.[52] We're unique, and thus each contribute to the total value of the world in a unique way. *How* are we unique, though? There may be more than one answer to this deep question. But here is one: we are unique, and uniquely valuable, in the personalities we enjoy. You have your own style. So do we. Those distinctive styles are good precisely because they are distinctive, and this is one reason why we enjoy non-fungible value.

The thought may be extended to God, if there is one. For God, one thinks, is special too, especially valuable, and even uniquely so (whether this is plausible without the assumption that God is a person too is hard to say). It's not as though we could replace the one true God with another maximally perfect being without loss of value. God, like us, enjoys non-fungible value. Could it be that God's special and non-fungible personal value derives, as ours does, in part from having a unique personality? We think so. But that thought may be

---

[50] Buckareff (2022, Section 2.3).   [51] Lebens (2015).   [52] Bailey and Rasmussen (2021).

sustained, obviously, only with the help of the hypothesis of divine personality. Thus, one more path from theism to personality.

Let's take stock. In earlier sections, we tore down barriers to accepting the hypothesis of divine personality. More recently, we have shown how that hypothesis bears on arguments for and against the existence of God, and that there are also ways of arguing from theism to personality. There is much we still haven't said, and many stones gestured at but left unturned. And yet this short study is most alarmingly approaching its terminus. Perhaps we owe readers an apology or two.

7 Encountering God

7.1 Apology

It is easy to go wrong when thinking about God, and very hard to get things right. It is especially easy to go wrong when thinking about God using only the tools of philosophy. God is big, and we are small. There are good reasons to think that our minds are ill-fitted to the task of figuring out divine matters all on their own. And yet doing something like that has been the task of the preceding pages. We have tried, using reason alone, to say some true and useful things about whether God could have a personality and what that might mean. You might think this is an issue. We're inclined to agree.

The feature identified here – roughly, that this has been an exercise in pure and unaided philosophical theology – has been made manifest in at least three related ways. First, we haven't actually said what God's personality is. We've given lots of candidate traits and used them as examples, but we haven't taken a stand on which ones God enjoys. We haven't even committed outright to the view that God has a personality: surprising and disappointing, one thinks, for an essay on divine personality. Second, we've operated at a highly abstract level, without tying things down to a particular Abrahamic faith, much less some specific tradition within it. We've thus declined to access the evidential riches, practical and doctrinal safety nets, and embedded wisdom of tradition. Third, we haven't even drawn from experience. The usual way to get to know a person is to spend time with them. But this hasn't been an essay that reports what we've learned about God through such communion. Nor has it been a guide for how others might pull off that task.

Here is our apology, working backwards through those three points. We think that one can learn who God is through communion – but the thing about communion is that no one else, including us, can do it for you. We think that working within a tradition is wise, and that both intellectual and spiritual errors may be avoided by doing so – but there are many traditions, and many ways to walk their paths. And with those two apologies in mind, it is less surprising that we haven't said who God is. This is something you're going to have to figure out yourself – within the bounds of your own home tradition, if you have one, and drawing on your own experience of God.

But all is not lost. Though we're philosophers, and though this remains a study in philosophical theology (and thus, not a study in scriptural theology or historical theology, nor a mystical handbook or treatise, devotional manual, guide to spiritual direction and soul care or interpretation of dreams), we have a few pointers for how to take things from here.

In particular, we're going to share a brief case study. It is situated within our own Christian tradition, and within one doctrinal and spiritual site where we think reflection on divine personality is likely to bear fruit: the Trinity. This is just a case study. Like the rest of this essay, it is somewhat speculative. But we hope it will illustrate one way forward for readers interested in knowing God. Perhaps, having considered the arguments of the preceding pages, you are newly open to the hypothesis of divine personality; we suggest that you find similar sites in your own home tradition, and work from there toward possible understanding of – or even acquaintance with – who God is.

7.2 God in Three Persons

According to Christians, though there is exactly one God, there are three divine persons – Father, Son, Holy Spirit. This is the doctrine of the Trinity. If true, the Trinity is not merely a doctrine. To say that God is three persons is to say who God is. And for this reason, we think, the Trinity is a prime site for reflection on divine personality, whether pursued with the tools of biblical, systematic, or historical theology, or even of mystical experience.

7.2.1 Three Divine Persons; Three Divine Personalities

There are three divine persons. Are there also three divine personalities? Does the Father have a personality distinct from that of the Son or Spirit? Do they all have personality traits? Which ones? The questions needn't be so abstract or tied to pure doctrine, either. We might add these, for example: does the Son prefer particular modes of communication that the Father does not? Should prayer directed toward the Spirit take special form to accommodate the Spirit's extroversion, which special form is not advisable when addressing the Father? Should we pray for comfort from the Spirit, but power from the Father, to match their unique preferred modes of interaction with us, preferences which reflect distinctive traits? Do Father, Son, and Spirit find different things funny or endearing?

Experience in conversation suggests that Christians divide nearly evenly in their reaction to these questions. To some, they don't make sense at all. The questions presuppose that there could be meaningful differences between, for example, Son and Spirit, and some find that idea to be more worthy of ridicule (or condemnation as heresy) than of careful consideration. Other Christians react quite differently; they say things like "you know, I've always felt closer to the Father than the Spirit, like we're more aligned in terms of how we prefer to pursue friendship; maybe my personality is more like the Father's than the Spirit's."

We have a guess as to what's going on here. When considering the Trinity, heresy looms twice over – tritheism on one side, modalism on the other. The edge of truth in the middle is so thin that many of us inevitably – and as a matter of personality, one might say – lean in one direction or the other. Christians naturally inclined toward the heresy of tritheism find internal distinction within the Trinity easy to accept and process. Christians naturally inclined toward the heresy of modalism find such distinctions rather difficult. Perhaps it all comes down to a difference of our own personalities.

This is not to concede that divine personality, specified further as the view that the Father, Son, and Spirit have different personalities, requires the heresy of tritheism. It is to speculate, rather, about which kind of Christian will be amenable to the idea: not heretics, but rather, orthodox Christians whose native disposition lies in the direction of one heresy rather than another.

We have occasionally emphasized the ways in which our topic is novel. Having situated it with respect to the Trinity, though, we're in a position to see that the topic is not entirely new. The way Christians think about our questions is by asking after differences between Father, Son, and Spirit, whether in the abstract, as when doing scholarly theology, or in more concrete ways as when engaging in corporate prayer or mystical communion with God. To do this just is, we suspect, to inquire into divine personality. If there turn out to be differences between Father, Son, and Spirit, they'll not pertain to classical perfections and the like. Rather, such differences will be more peculiar and, well, personal – traits and their consequences.

Theologians are quick to emphasize that "person" in Trinitarian formulas does not mean what it does in more colloquial contexts. To say that the Father is a different person than the Spirit isn't the same as saying Maya is a different person than Duncan – blessed with different druthers and delights, drawn to different styles of artistic expression, and so on. But maybe those theologians were too quick in their strictures. And maybe we were too quick to accept them all at face value. Maybe the Father and the Son differ with respect to their favored colors or modes of communication. Maybe the Trinity is precisely where we find, not one divine personality, but three.

7.2.2 "Myself"

To get a feel for how investigation into three divine personalities might go, let's look at some classic children's fantasy literature. Consider this passage from C. S. Lewis' *A Horse and His Boy* (we'll keep it brief; but for full effect, we suggest that you read the full book; it's a good yarn and worth the time):

> "Who are you?" asked Shasta.
> "Myself," said the Voice, very deep and low so that the earth shook: and again "Myself," loud and clear and gay: and then the third time "Myself," whispered so softly you could hardly hear it, and yet it seemed to come from all round you as if the leaves rustled with it.[53]

Shasta is here asking, not what, but *who* God is. He gets three answers. The first is an expression of creative might. This is the Father. The second, embodied joy. This is the Son. The third, subtle energy. This is the Spirit. We think a personality interpretation fits nicely with this passage. Who is God? God is three divine persons, three people who differ in who they are, and also in how they present themselves. They communicate in different ways. Interactions with them differ in dominant emotional note. Different people, different vibes. Of course they do not disagree with each other; their answers to the question are the same in substance ("Myself"). But they differ in flavor, in personality.

We do not say that this interpretation is forced by the target passage. But it is certainly permitted by it. And having observed our technique, we suspect you'll find other ways to apply it. In short: look for places in Christian thinking – or experience or theology or speculation or even fiction – where the Trinity and variation across its three persons are explicitly in view, and there find evidence of three divine personalities and details about how they differ.

That God might show up in one place in three very different ways is not a new idea. It is as old as the story of Jesus' baptism and the three divine persons there on display: a man in the water, a voice in heaven, and a spirit somehow like a dove. For Christians, the Trinity is everywhere. So too, we suggest, three divine personalities.

7.2.3 Taste and See

Of course the Trinity is not just a doctrine. It is, if Christians are to be believed, a rather important reality. Books, no matter their genre, are not the only tool we have by which to approach that reality. Indeed, taking God's personality seriously requires that we attend carefully to God's own preferences about how to be approached, and for some it will be an open and important question whether those preferences vary across Father, Son, and Spirit.

---

[53] Lewis (1954/2001, pp. 113–114).

Can the Christian come to know three divine personalities, not in studying Scripture or C. S. Lewis' stories or theological treatises on the three divine persons, but in rather more *engaged* or *practical* ways? Indeed they can. They can try, at least. Here are some ideas as to how that might work. They will require significant modulation to make sense across various Christian traditions, and even more modulation if extended to other theistic religious traditions. They are not arguments, nor are they unqualified spiritual advice; they are, rather, illustrations of how one might proceed, if one wished to proceed in this way. And as you consider them, remember: we're just a couple of philosophers.[54]

If you're a praying Christian, keep track of who you are praying to. Experiment, within the bounds of correct doctrine and practice. Take effort to notice what happens. Do you feel as though you're encountering a different person – a different personality – when addressing the Father vs. the Son? Do you feel the Spirit's pleasure shine on you when you recall certain jokes, but not others? Do you feel more drawn to one member of the Trinity than to the others? How so? Does it make a difference whether you are praying in community or alone?

If you're a worshiping Christian, keep track of who you're worshiping. Can you detect differing emotional notes in any divine response? Which kinds of hymns or psalms or spiritual songs please the Son most of all? Are certain saints more present in some settings than in others? How could you tell? And if you're really serious about all this, do it in the context of a community of thoughtful believers and its repositories of wisdom. It is dangerous to go alone; so don't.

If you're a reading Christian, read the book of Jonah, and feel free to, with THE LORD, laugh at the antics therein. Might this book be configured in this curious way (and it is curious) both for our delight, and to disclose a distinctive sense of humor? Whose sense of humor is in view – the Father's? What is it like? Does the divine person on display in the book of Jonah evince a particular style of communication? How so? Consider, too, Jesus of Nazareth as depicted in the Gospel of Mark. This Jesus says and does weird things, and sometimes appears to be toying with his disciples and the crowds that follow. This Jesus hides – behind words and riddles, or even in a boat. Some of this might reflect, of course, the personality of that Gospel's author. But might it say something, too, about the second person of the Trinity? What kind of a person – endowed with what kind of personality – might opt to communicate or move in these weird ways? One can, of course, repeat this exercise with other books of Scripture, and indeed with other books as well, provided one has reason to think they contain wisdom – even children's fantasy.

---

[54] See also Stump (2010) and (2012).

Here is a slogan to keep in mind throughout: trust but verify. Verify our speculations by finding God yourself – Father, Son, and Holy Spirit. A posture of faith or trust – not in us, nor even in yourself, but in God – may be an important ingredient here too.[55] And fidelity to the Church must, according to some traditions, play a powerful governing role in how any of these activities unfold.

Maybe, after all of that, you'll come to the conclusion that God doesn't have a personality, or that the persons of the Trinity do not have distinct personalities. No harm, we say – at least you'll have prayed and worshiped and read a bit.

But maybe, just maybe, you'll taste and see that THE LORD is weird.

7.3 God the Artist

It's time to zoom out. All the way out. Imagine the entirety of the cosmos spread before you: quasars, galaxies, the whole shebang. This is God's work. It is bold, and weird, and lovely, and full of detail and character. One could get lost here.

The cosmos is a work of art. It is *the* work of art. God is the artist.

You could encounter God through doctrine – as when reading ponderous tomes of philosophical theology. This is like reading about a great artist. You could encounter God through practice – as when praying, and as discussed above. This is like speaking to the artist in person, or perhaps like taking her on as an unusually distant pen pal.

Between these two poles lies a third way of encountering an artist: not conversation or correspondence, and not inference from interpretive essays, but rather in experience of what she has made. This is one way to become acquainted with the personality of an artist. Study her work. Know its creative ambitions. Love it with your patient attention. Let its style confuse or delight, as the case may be – and in time, you'll see who she is. For creative style, when done right, is far more than formula-following. It is personality-disclosing. The poet Frank O'Hara reportedly put the point this way: "Style at its lowest ebb is method. Style at its highest ebb is personality."[56]

Have you done this, with a great piece of music, a story, a film? Encountered it so deeply that you feel you've come to understand who made it? If so, then you know what we're going to say next.

If you are interested in knowing who God is, and newly open to the hypothesis of divine personality, this idea is for you: study the cosmos. Get lost within its details. Love it with your patient attention. The path from these details to conclusions about its maker will never be straight and easy.[57] Nor is it the only or main point of study, any more than it is in the case of a creaturely artist and

---

[55] Page (2017).   [56] As quoted in Bennett (2019, p. 130).   [57] Brassey (2019).

her work. But if we're right – if the cosmos is a work of art, and if art reveals the traits of its maker – there are lessons here, for anyone who wishes to find them.

Study the cosmos. Know God.[58]

There's a word for people who study the cosmos. We call them *scientists*. Sometimes scientists uncover deep and elegant unity, as when finding gravitational rules that govern both planets and pens. But sometimes their discoveries are more curious or downright funny (if you don't think lobsters are funny, consider the platypus). Discoveries like these remind us: the cosmos is a weird place. Perhaps its maker hopes to make us gape, or even to laugh.[59] Our world is blessed with nooks and crannies and hilarious odds and ends. To come to know them is nothing less than to encounter a strange and untamed God.

---

[58] Benton (2024, Sections 4–5).   [59] Peels (2015).

References

Adams, Marilyn McCord (1999). *Horrendous Evils and the Goodness of God.* Oxford University Press.

Alston, William P. (1993). Aquinas on Theological Predication. In Eleonore Stump, ed., *Reasoned Faith: Essays in Philosophical Theology in Honor of Norman Kretzmann.* Cornell University Press, pp. 145–178.

Amijee, Fatema (2022a). Inquiry and Metaphysical Rationalism. *Australasian Journal of Philosophy* 101 (4): 809–823.

Amijee, Fatema (2022b). The Contingency of Creation and Divine Choice. *Oxford Studies in Philosophy of Religion* 10: 289–300.

Axinn, Sidney (1990). Moral Style. *Journal of Value Inquiry* 24: 123–133.

Bailey, Andrew M. (2021). *Monotheism and Human Nature.* Cambridge University Press.

Bailey, Andrew M. and Joshua Rasmussen (2021). How Valuable Could a Person Be? *Philosophy & Phenomenological Research* 103: 264–277.

Bennett, Chad (2019). *Word of Mouth.* Johns Hopkins University Press.

Benton, Matthew (2024). *Knowledge and God.* Cambridge University Press.

Bergmann, Michael (2001). Skeptical Theism and Rowe's New Evidential Argument from Evil. *Noûs* 35 (2): 278–296.

Bergmann, Michael (2021). Skeptical Theism and Rowe's New Evidential Argument from Evil. *Noûs* 35: 278–296.

Brassey, Vanessa (2019). The Implied Painter. *Debates in Aesthetics* 14: 15–29.

Buchak, Lara (2013). *Risk and Rationality.* Oxford University Press.

Buckareff, Andrei A. (2022). *Pantheism.* Cambridge University Press.

Burns, Elizabeth (2009). Must Theists Believe in a Personal God? *Think* 8: 77–86.

Burns, Elizabeth (2015). Classical and Revisionary Theism on the Divine as Personal: A Rapprochement? *International Journal for Philosophy of Religion* 78: 151–165.

Chang, Ruth (1997). Introduction. In Ruth Chang, ed., *Incommensurability, Incomparability, and Practical Reason.* Harvard University Press, pp. 1–41.

Chang, Ruth (2002). The Possibility of Parity. *Ethics* 112: 659–688.

Cloninger, Susan (2009). Conceptual Issues in Personality Theory. In Philip J. Corr and Gerald Matthews, eds., *The Cambridge Handbook of Personality Psychology.* Cambridge University Press, pp. 3–26.

Davies, Brian (2004). *An Introduction to the Philosophy of Religion,* 3rd ed. Oxford University Press.

Flores, Carolina (2021). Epistemic Styles. *Philosophical Topics* 49: 35–55.

Horowitz, Sophie (2019). The Truth Problem for Permissivism. *Journal of Philosophy* 116 (5): 237–262.

Howard-Snyder, Daniel (1996). The Argument from Inscrutable Evil. In Daniel Howard-Snyder, ed., *The Evidential Argument from Evil*. Indiana University Press, pp. 286–310.

Hudson, Hud (2014). The Father of Lies? *Oxford Studies in Philosophy of Religion* 5: 147–166.

Keller, Lorraine Juliano (2018). Divine Ineffability and Franciscan Knowledge. *Res Philosophica* 95: 347–370.

Kvanvig, Jonathan (2022). *Depicting Deity: A Metatheological Approach*. Oxford University Press.

Lebens, Samuel (2015). God and His Imaginary Friends: A Hassidic Metaphysics. *Religious Studies* 51: 183–204.

Lewis, Clive Staples (1954/2001). *A Horse and His Boy*. Harper Collins.

Mander, William J. (1997). God and Personality. *Heythrop Journal* 38: 401–412.

Mooney, Justin (2019). From a Cosmic Fine-Tuner to a Perfect Being. *Analysis* 79: 449–452.

Mullins, Ryan (2020). *God and Emotion*. Cambridge University Press.

Murphy, Mark (2011). *God and Moral Law: On the Theistic Explanation of Morality*. Oxford University Press.

Nagasawa, Yujin (2017). *Maximal God*. Oxford University Press.

O'Connor, Timothy (2004). And This All Men Call God. *Faith and Philosophy* 21: 417–435.

Oppy, Graham (2014). Ultimate Naturalistic Causal Explanation. In Tyrone Goldschmidt, ed., *The Puzzle of Existence: Why Is There Something Rather than Nothing?* Routledge, pp. 46–63.

Page, Meghan (2017). The Posture of Faith. *Oxford Studies in Philosophy of Religion* 8: 227–244.

Peels, Rik (2015). Does God Have a Sense of Humor? *Faith and Philosophy* 32 (3): 271–292.

Plantinga, Alvin (2007). Two Dozen (or so) Theistic Arguments. In Deane-Peter Baker, ed., *Alvin Plantinga*. Cambridge University Press, pp. 203–227.

Pruss, Alexander (2006). *The Principle of Sufficient Reason*. Cambridge University Press.

Pruss, Alexander (2016). Divine Creative Freedom. *Oxford Studies in Philosophy of Religion* 7: 213–238.

Rasmussen, Joshua (2009). From a Necessary Being to God. *International Journal for Philosophy of Religion* 66: 1–13.

Rea, Michael C. (2011). Divine Hiddenness, Divine Silence. In Louis P. Pojman and Michael C. Rea, eds., *Philosophy of Religion: An Anthology*. Wadsworth/ Cengage, pp. 266–275.

Rea, Michael C. (2016). Gender as a Divine Attribute. *Religious Studies* 52: 97–115.

Rea, Michael C. (2018). *The Hiddenness of God*. Oxford University Press.

Rettler, Bradley (forthcoming). The Presence of Evil and the Absence of God. In David Friedell, ed., *The Philosophy of Ted Chiang*. Palgrave MacMillan.

Rettler, Bradley and Ryan Matthew Parker (2017). A Possible Worlds Solution to the Puzzle of Petitionary Prayer. *European Journal for Philosophy of Religion* 9: 178–186.

Rettler, Bradley and Andrew M. Bailey (2023). Object. In Edward N. Zalta and Uri Nodelman, eds., *Stanford Encyclopedia of Philosophy*. https://plato.stan ford.edu/entries/object/.

Riggle, Nick (2015). Personal Style and Artistic Style. *Philosophical Quarterly* 65: 711–731.

Robinson, Jenefer (1984). Style and Personality in the Literary Work. *The Philosophical Review* 94: 227–247.

Ross, Stephanie (2005). Style in Art. In Jerrold Levinson, ed., *The Oxford Handbook of Aesthetics*. Oxford University Press, pp. 228–244.

Schoenfield, Miriam (2014). Permission to Believe: Why Permissivism Is True and What It Tells Us about Irrelevant Influences on Belief. *Noûs* 48: 193–218.

Speaks, Jeff (2018). *The Greatest Possible Being*. Oxford University Press.

Stump, Eleonore (2010). *Wandering in Darkness: Narrative and the Problem of Suffering*. Oxford University Press.

Stump, Eleonore (2012). Wandering in Darkness: Further Reflections. *European Journal for Philosophy of Religion* 4 (3): 197–219.

Sullivan, Meghan (2019). *Time Biases*. Oxford University Press.

Thornton, Allison Krile (2023). Petitionary Prayer: Wanting to Change the Mind of the Being Who Knows Best. *Faith and Philosophy* 39: 227–242.

van Inwagen, Peter (2015). *Metaphysics*. Westview Press.

Ward, Thomas (2020). *Divine Ideas*. Cambridge University Press.

Willard, Dallas (1997). *The Divine Conspiracy*. Harper Collins.

Wilson, Jessica (2023). Determinables and Determinates. In Edward N. Zalta and Uri Nodelman, eds., *Stanford Encyclopedia of Philosophy*. https://plato .stanford.edu/archives/spr2023/entries/determinate-determinables/.

Woolard, Fiona (2016). Dimensions of Demandingness. *Proceedings of the Aristotelian Society* 116: 89–106.

Acknowledgments

There are exactly two block quotations in this study. One's author is the person to whom we dedicate the work: Mike Rea – our teacher, our mentor, our friend.

For helpful conversation or comments, we thank anonymous referees, the editors, Alex Arnold, Robert Audi, Jeffrey Brower, Laura Frances Callahan, Brian Cutter, Grace Hibshman, Dominic LaMantia, Sam Newlands, Katie O'Dell, Stephen Ogden, Ciara O'Rourke, Andrew Peterson, Josh Rasmussen, Mike Rea, Noël Saenz, Fred Sanders, Mack Sullivan, Katherine Sweet, Meredith Trexler Drees, Johnny Waldrop, Andreas Waldstein, Fritz Warfield, Scott Williams, Craig Warmke, Josh Wong, and Eric Yang. We also thank the Center for Philosophy of Religion at the University of Notre Dame, Yale-NUS College, and the College of Arts & Sciences at the University of Wyoming for research support. At a conference at Notre Dame in 2009, Hud Hudson asked, "Which person of the Trinity has played the most important role in your coming to whatever relationship you currently have with God?" The question bore fruit, some of which is in the essay you have just finished reading. Thank you, Hud, for your questions and for prompting us long ago to start thinking about divine personality.

Cambridge Elements ⹀

The Problems of God

Series Editor
Michael L. Peterson
Asbury Theological Seminary

Michael L. Peterson is Professor of Philosophy at Asbury Theological Seminary. He is the author of *God and Evil* (Routledge); *Monotheism, Suffering, and Evil* (Cambridge University Press); *With All Your Mind* (University of Notre Dame Press); *C. S. Lewis and the Christian Worldview* (Oxford University Press); *Evil and the Christian God* (Baker Book House); and *Philosophy of Education: Issues and Options* (Intervarsity Press). He is co-author of *Reason and Religious Belief* (Oxford University Press); *Science, Evolution, and Religion: A Debate about Atheism and Theism* (Oxford University Press); and *Biology, Religion, and Philosophy* (Cambridge University Press). He is editor of *The Problem of Evil: Selected Readings* (University of Notre Dame Press). He is co-editor of *Philosophy of Religion: Selected Readings* (Oxford University Press) and *Contemporary Debates in Philosophy of Religion* (Wiley-Blackwell). He served as General Editor of the Blackwell monograph series Exploring Philosophy of Religion and is founding Managing Editor of the journal *Faith and Philosophy*.

About the Series
This series explores problems related to God, such as the human quest for God or gods, contemplation of God, and critique and rejection of God. Concise, authoritative volumes in this series will reflect the methods of a variety of disciplines, including philosophy of religion, theology, religious studies, and sociology.

Cambridge Elements ≡

The Problems of God

Printed in the United States
by Baker & Taylor Publisher Services